IN THE YULE-LOG GLOW

Book III

Various Authors

CHRISTMAS POEMS FROM 'ROUND THE WORLD

"Sic as folk tell ower at a winter ingle"

Scott

THREE VOLUMES IN ONE

Editor: **Harrison S. Morris**

[ZHINGOORA BOOKS]

BETWEEN THE TALE-TELLING.

Fancy, if you will, Gentle Reader, that, between the intervals of tale-telling,—the Yule-log still ruddy upon the visages of your fellow-guests from many lands,—fancy that a quiet traveller draws out of his side-pocket a little, well-worn pair of books from which he reads some scrap of verse or some melodious Christmas poem. Fancy, too, that, beneath the inn windows, in the snow outside, an occasional band of the Waits strikes up an ancient carol with voice and horn, begging, when the music is done, admittance to the glowing warmth within doors and a share in the plenteous cakes and ale.

Imagine this, if you will, and choose, from the pages to come, whatever of old or new will fit well into the conceit; for not a few carols or legends lie there which have done service under the snow-covered gables or by the crackling wood, and which will help, with their quaint heartiness or simple beauty, to realize the charm of Christmas the world around,—that charm which flows from hearty and generous good-will towards men; which has for its inner light the kindly desire for peace on earth.

CONTENTS OF BOOK III.

Saint Distaff's Day, the
Morrow after Twelfth Day

The Shepherds.

On Oaten Pipes

Pipe-Playing

The First Carol

In Bethlehem

A Carol in the Pastures

The Shepherds

On Shepherds' Pipes

Angel Tidings

The News-Bearers

Hymn for Christmas-Day

A Hymn of the Nativity

Sung by the Shepherd

From "The Light of the World"[C]

It Brings Good Cheer.

Old Christmas Returned

The Trencherman

Ban and Blessing

Thrice Welcome!

Christmas Provender

Glee and Solace

On Saint John's Day

Christmas Alms

Christmas at the Round-Table

Lullaby.

A Carol at the Manger

A Dream Carol

The King in the Cradle

Madonna and Child

A Rocking Hymn

A Cradle-Song of the Virgin

Whispering Palms

A Christmas Lullaby

The Virgin's Cradle-Hymn

The Sovereign

By the Cradle-Side

The Virgin Mary to the Child
Jesus

A Bedside Ditty

Given Back on Christmas
Morn

A Lulling Song

Good-Night

FOOTNOTES:

[A] By the courtesy of Messrs. Houghton, Mifflin & Co.

[B] By the courtesy of The Century Company.

[C] By the courtesy of Messrs. Funk & Wagnalls.

Legends in Song.

"Tell sweet old tales, Sing songs as we sit bending o'er the hearth, Till the lamp flickers and the memory fails."

Frederick Tennyson.

THE HALLOWED TIME.

Some say that ever 'gainst that season comesWherein our Saviour's birth is celebrated,The bird of dawning singeth all night long;And then, they say, no spirit dares stir abroad;The nights are wholesome, then no planets strike,No fairy takes, nor witch hath power to charm,So hallowed and so gracious is the time.

Shakespeare.

ON THE MORNING OF CHRIST'S NATIVITY.

This is the month, and this the happy morn, Wherein the Son of Heaven's eternal King, Of wedded maid and virgin mother born, Our great redemption from above did bring; For so the holy sages once did sing, That he our deadly forfeit should release, And with his Father work us a perpetual peace.

That glorious form, that light insufferable, And that far-beaming blaze of majesty, Wherewith he wont at heaven's high council-table To sit the midst of Trinal Unity, He laid aside; and, here with us to be, Forsook the courts of everlasting day, And chose with us a darksome house of mortal clay.

Say, heavenly Muse, shall not thy sacred vein Afford a present to the Infant-God? Hast thou no verse, no hymn, or solemn strain To welcome him to this his new abode, Now while the heaven, by the sun's team untrod, Hath took no print of the approaching light, And all the spangled host kept watch in squadron bright?

See, how from far, upon the eastern road, The star-led wizards haste with odors sweet; O run, prevent them with thy humble ode, And lay it lowly at his blessed feet; Have thou the honor first thy Lord to greet, And join thy voice unto the angel-quire, From out his secret altar touch'd with hallow'd fire.

THE HYMN.

It was the winter wild,While the heaven-born ChildAll meanly wrapt in the rude manger lies;Nature in awe to him,Had doff'd her gaudy trim,With her great Master so to sympathize:It was no season then for herTo wanton with the sun, her lusty paramour.

Only with speeches fairShe woos the gentle airTo hide her guilty front with innocent snow;And on her naked shame,Pollute with sinful blame,The saintly veil of maiden-white to throw;Confounded, that her Maker's eyesShould look so near upon her foul deformities.

But he, her fears to cease,Sent down the meek-eyed Peace;She, crown'd with olive green, came softly slidingDown through the turning sphere,His ready Harbinger,With turtle wing the amorous clouds dividing;And, waving wide her myrtle wand,She strikes an universal peace through sea and land.

No war, or battle's soundWas heard the world around;The idle spear and shield were high up-hung;The hooked chariot stoodUnstain'd with hostile blood;The trumpet spake not to the armed throng;And kings sat still with awful eye,As if they surely knew their sovereign Lord was by.

But peaceful was the nightWherein the Prince of LightHis reign of peace upon the earth began:The winds, with wonder whist,Smoothly the waters kist,Whispering new joys to the mild

14

ocean, Who now hath quite forgot to rave, While birds of calm sit brooding on the charmed wave.

The stars, with deep amaze, Stand fix'd in steadfast gaze, Bending one way their precious influence; And will not take their flight, For all the morning light, Or Lucifer that often warn'd them thence; But in their glimmering orbs did glow, Until their Lord himself bespake, and bid them go.

And, though the shady gloomHad given day her room, The sun himself withheld his wonted speed, And hid his head for shame, As his inferior flameThe new-enlighten'd world no more should need. He saw a greater Sun appearThan his bright throne, or burning axletree, could bear.

The shepherds on the lawn, Or e'er the point of dawn, Sat simply chatting in a rustic row; Full little thought they thenThat the mighty PanWas kindly come to live with them below; Perhaps their loves, or else their sheep, Was all that did their silly thoughts so busy keep.

When such music sweetTheir hearts and ears did greet, As never was by mortal fingers strook; Divinely-warbled voiceAnswering the stringed noise, As all their souls in blissful rapture took; The air, such pleasure loth to lose, With thousand echoes still prolongs each heavenly close.

Nature that heard such sound, Beneath the hollow roundOf Cynthia's seat, the airy region thrilling, Now was almost wonTo think her part was done, And that her reign had here its last fulfilling;She knew such harmony aloneCould hold all heaven and earth in happier union.

At last surrounds their sightA globe of circular light,That with long beams the shame-faced night array'd;The helmed cherubim,And sworded seraphim,Are seen in glittering ranks with wings display'd,Harping in loud and solemn quire,With unexpressive notes, to Heaven's new-born Heir.

Such music as, 'tis said,Before was never made,But when of old the sons of morning sung,While the Creator greatHis constellations set,And the well-balanced world on hinges hung,And cast the dark foundations deep,And bid the weltering waves their oozy channel keep.

Ring out, ye crystal spheres,Once bless our human ears,If ye have power to touch our senses so;And let your silver chimeMove in melodious time,And let the base of Heaven's deep organ blow,And, with your ninefold harmony,Make up full concert to the angelic symphony.

For, if such holy songEnwrap our fancy long,Time will run back and fetch the age of gold,And speckled VanityWill sicken soon and die,And leprous Sin will melt from earthly mould,And Hell itself will pass away,And leave her dolorous mansions to the peering day.

Yea, Truth and Justice thenWill down return to men,Orb'd in a rainbow; and, like glories wearing,Mercy will sit between,Throned in celestial sheen,With radiant feet the tissued clouds down steering;And Heaven, as at some festival,Will open wide the gates of her high palace-hall.

But wisest Fate says No,This must not yet be so;The Babe lies yet in smiling infancy,That on the bitter crossMust redeem our loss,So both himself and us to glorify:Yet first, to those ychain'd in sleep,The wakeful trump of doom must thunder through the deep;

With such a horrid clangAs on Mount Sinai rang,While the red fire and smouldering clouds outbreak:The aged earth aghastWith terror of that blast,Shall from the surface to the centre shake;When at the world's last session,The dreadful Judge in middle air shall spread his throne.

And then at last our blissFull and perfect is,But now begins; for, from this happy day,The Old Dragon, under groundIn straighter limits bound,Not half so far casts his usurped sway;And, wroth to see his kingdom fail,Swinges the scaly horror of his folded tail.

The oracles are dumb,No voice or hideous humRuns through the arched roof in words deceiving.Apollo from his shrineCan no more divine,With hollow shriek the steep of Delphos leaving.No nightly trance, or breathed spell,Inspires the pale-eyed priest from the prophetic cell.

The lonely mountains o'er,And the resounding shore,A voice of weeping heard and loud lament;From haunted spring and dale,Edged with poplar pale,The parting Genius is with sighing sent;With flower-inwoven tresses torn,The Nymphs in twilight shade of tangled thickets, mourn.

In consecrated earth,And on the holy hearth,The Lars and Lemures moan with midnight plaint;In urns, and altars round,A drear and dying soundAffrights the Flamens at their service quaint;And the chill marble seems to sweat,While each peculiar power foregoes his wonted seat.

Peor and BaälimForsake their temples dim,With that twice-batter'd god of Palestine;And mooned Ashtaroth,Heaven's queen and mother both,Now sits not girt with tapers' holy shine;The Lybic Hammon shrinks his horn,In vain the Tyrian maids their wounded Thammuz mourn.

And sullen Moloch, fled,Hath left in shadows dreadHis burning idol all of blackest hue;In vain with cymbals' ringThey call the grisly king,In dismal dance about the furnace blue;The brutish gods of Nile as fast,Isis, and Orus, and the dog Anubis, haste.

Nor is Osiris seenIn Memphian grove or green,Trampling the unshower'd grass with lowings loud:Nor can he be at restWithin his sacred chest;Naught but profoundest hell can be his shroud;In vain, with timbrell'd anthems dark,The sable-stoled sorcerers bear his worshipt ark.

He feels from Judah's landThe dreaded Infant's hand,The rays of Bethlehem blind his dusky eyn;Nor all the gods besideLonger dare abide,Nor Typhon huge ending in snaky twine;Our Babe, to show his Godhead true,Can in his swaddling-bands control the damned crew.

So, when the sun in bed,Curtain'd with cloudy red,Pillows his chin upon an orient wave,The flocking shadows paleTroop to the infernal jail,Each fetter'd ghost slips to his several grave;And the yellow-skirted faysFly after the night-steeds, leaving their moon-loved maze.

But see, the Virgin blestHath laid her Babe to rest;Time is our tedious song should here have ending:Heaven's youngest teemed starHath fix'd her polished car,Her sleeping Lord, with handmaid lamp attending:And all about the courtly stableBright-harnessed angels sit in order serviceable.

John Milton.

THE FIRST ROMAN CHRISTMAS.

It was the calm and silent night!Seven hundred years and fifty-threeHad Rome been growing up to might,And now was queen of land and sea.No sound was heard of clashing wars,Peace brooded o'er the hushed domain;Apollo, Pallas, Jove, and MarsHeld undisturbed their ancient reign,In the solemn midnightCenturies ago.

'Twas in the calm and silent night!The senator of haughty RomeImpatient urged his chariot's flight,From lonely revel rolling home.Triumphal arches, gleaming, swellHis breast with thoughts of boundless sway;What recked the Roman what befellA paltry province far awayIn the solemn midnightCenturies ago?

Within that province far awayWent plodding home a weary boor;A streak of light before him lay,Fallen through a half-shut stable-door,Across his path. He passed; for naughtTold what was going on within.How keen the stars! his only thought;The air how calm, and cold, and thin!In the solemn midnightCenturies ago.

O strange indifference! Low and highDrowsed over common joys and cares;The earth was still, but knew not why;The world was listening unawares.How calm a moment may precedeOne that shall thrill the world forever!To that still moment none would heed,Man's doom was linked, no more to sever,In the solemn midnightCenturies ago.

It is the calm and solemn night!A thousand bells ring out and throwTheir joyous peals abroad, and smiteThe darkness, charmed, and holy now!The night that erst no name had worn,To it a happy name is given;For in that stable lay, new-born,The peaceful Prince of earth and heaven,In the solemn midnightCenturies ago.

Alfred H. Domett.

THE THREE DAMSELS.

(SUGGESTED BY A DRAWING OF DANTE GABRIEL ROSSETTI'S.)

Three damsels in the queen's chamber, The queen's mouth was most fair; She spake a word of God's mother As the combs went in her hair. Mary that is of might, Bring us to thy Son's sight.

They held the gold combs out from her A span's length off her head; She sang this song of God's mother And of her bearing-bed. Mary most full of grace, Bring us to thy Son's face.

When she sat at Joseph's hand, She looked against her side; And either way from the short silk band Her girdle was all wried. Mary that all good may, Bring us to thy Son's way.

Mary had three women for her bed, The twain were maidens clean; The first of them had white and red, The third had riven green. Mary that is so sweet, Bring us to thy Son's feet.

She had three women for her hair, Two were gloved soft and shod; The third had feet and fingers bare, She was the likest God. Mary that wieldeth land, Bring us to thy Son's hand.

She had three women for her ease, The twain were good women; The first two were the two Maries, The third was Magdalen. Mary that perfect is, Bring us to thy Son's kiss.

Joseph had three workmen in his stall, To serve him well upon; The first of them were Peter and Paul, The third of them was John. Mary, God's handmaiden, Bring us to thy Son's ken.

"If your child be none other man's, But if it be very mine, The bedstead shall be gold two spans, The bed-foot silver fine." Mary that made God mirth, Bring us to thy Son's birth.

"If the child be some other man's, And if it be none of mine, The manger shall be straw two spans, Betwixen kine and kine." Mary that made sin cease, Bring us to thy Son's peace.

Christ was born upon this wise: It fell on such a night, Neither with sounds of psalteries, Nor with fire for light. Mary that is God's spouse, Bring us to thy Son's house.

The star came out upon the east With a great sound and sweet: Kings gave gold to make him feast And myrrh for him to eat. Mary of thy sweet mood, Bring us to thy Son's good.

He had two handmaids at his head, One handmaid at his feet; The twain of them were fair and red, The third one was right sweet. Mary that is most wise, Bring us to thy Son's eyes. Amen.

Algernon Charles Swinburne.

KING OLAF'S CHRISTMAS.

At Drontheim, Olaf the KingHeard the bells of Yule-tide ring,As he sat in his banquet hall,Drinking the nut-brown ale,With his bearded Berserks haleAnd tall.

Three days his Yule-tide feastsHe held with Bishops and Priests,And his horn filled up to the brim;But the ale was never too strong,Nor the Sagaman's tale too long,For him.

O'er his drinking-horn, the signHe made of the cross divineAs he drank, and muttered his prayers;But the Berserks evermoreMade the sign of the Hammer of ThorOver theirs.

The gleams of the fire-light danceUpon helmet and hauberk and lanceAnd laugh in the eyes of the king;And he cries to Halfred the Scald,Gray-bearded, wrinkled, and bald:"Sing!

"Sing me a song divine,With a sword in every line,And this shall be thy reward;"And he loosened the belt at his waist,And in front of the singer placedHis sword.

"Quern-biter of Hakon the Good,Wherewith at a stroke he hewedThe millstone through and through,And Foot-breadth of Thoralf the StrongWere neither so broad nor so longNor so true."

Then the Scald took his harp and sang,And loud through the music rangThe sound of that shining word;And the harp-strings a clangor madeAs if they were struck with the bladeOf a sword.

And the Berserks round aboutBroke forth into a shoutThat made the rafters ring;They smote with their fists on the board,And shouted, "Long live the swordAnd the King!"

But the king said, "O my son,I miss the bright word in oneOf thy measures and thy rhymes."And Halfred the Scald replied,"In another 'twas multipliedThree times."

Then King Olaf raised the hiltOf iron, cross-shaped and gilt,And said, "Do not refuse;Count well the gain and the loss,Thor's hammer or Christ's cross:Choose!"

And Halfred the Scald said, "This,In the name of the Lord, I kiss,Who on it was crucified!"And a shout went round the board,"In the name of Christ the LordWho died!"

Then over the waste of snowsThe noonday sun uproseThrough the driving mists revealed,Like the lifting of the Host,By incense-clouds almostConcealed.

On the shining wall a vastAnd shadowy cross was castFrom the hilt of the lifted sword,And in foaming cups of aleThe Berserks drank "Was-hael!To the Lord!"

Henry Wadsworth Longfellow.

HALBERT AND HOB.

Here is a thing that happened. Like wild beasts whelped, for den, In a wild part of North England, there lived once two wild men, Inhabiting one homestead, neither a hovel nor hut, Time out of mind their birthright: father and son, these,—but,—Such a son, such a father! Most wildness by degrees Softens away: yet, last of their line, the wildest and worst were these.

Criminals, then? Why, no: they did not murder and rob; But give them a word, they returned a blow,—old Halbert as young Hob: Harsh and fierce of word, rough and savage of deed, Hated or feared the more—who knows?—the genuine wild-beast breed.

Thus were they found by the few sparse folk of the country-side; But how fared each with other? E'en beasts couch, hide by hide. In a growling, grudged agreement: so father son lay curled The closelier up in their den because the last of their kind in the world.

Still, beast irks beast on occasion. One Christmas night of snow, Came father and son to words—such words! more cruel because the blow To crown each word was wanting, while taunt matched gibe, and curse Competed with oath in wager, like pastime in hell,—nay, worse: For pastime turned to earnest, as up there sprang at last The son at the throat of the father, seized him, and held him fast.

"Out of this house you go!"—there followed a hideous oath—"This oven where now we bake, too hot to hold us both! If there's snow outside, there's coolness: out with you, bide a spellin the drift, and save the sexton the charge of a parish shell!"

Now, the old trunk was tough, was solid as stump of oakUntouched at the core by a thousand years: much less had its seventy brokeOne whipcord nerve in the muscly mass from neck to shoulder-bladeOf the mountainous man, whereon his child's rash hand like a feather weighed.

Nevertheless at once did the mammoth shut his eyes,Drop chin to breast, drop hands to sides, stand stiffened,—arms and thighsAll of a piece—struck mute, much as a sentry stands,Patient to take the enemy's fire: his captain so commands.

Whereat the son's wrath flew to fury at such sheer scornOf his puny strength by the giant eld thus acting the babe new-born:And "Neither will this turn serve!" yelled he. "Out with you! Trundle, log!If you cannot tramp and trudge like a man, try all-fours like a dog!"

Still the old man stood mute. So, logwise,—down to floorPulled from his fireside place, dragged on from hearth to door,—Was he pushed, a very log, staircase along, untilA certain turn in the steps was reached, a yard from the house-door sill.

Then the father opened his eyes,—each spark of their rage extinct,—Temples, late black, dead-blanched, right-hand with left-hand linked,—He faced his son submissive; when slow the accents came,They were strangely mild though his son's rash hand on his neck lay all the same.

"Halbert, on such a night of a Christmas long ago,For such a cause, with such a gesture, did I drag—so—My father down thus far: but, softening here, I heardA voice in my heart, and stopped: you wait for an outer word.

"For your own sake, not mine, soften you too! UntrodLeave this last step we reach, nor brave the finger of God!I dared not pass its lifting: I did well. I nor blameNor praise you. I stopped here: Halbert, do you the same!"

Straightway the son relaxed his hold of the father's throat.They mounted, side by side, to the room again: no noteTook either of each, no sign made each to either: lastAs first, in absolute silence, their Christmas-night they passed.

At dawn, the father sate on, dead, in the selfsame place,With an outburst blackening still the old bad fighting-face:But the son crouched all a-tremble like any lamb new-yeaned.

When he went to the burial, some one's staff he borrowed,—tottered and leaned.But his lips were loose, not locked,—kept muttering, mumbling. "There!At his cursing and swearing!" the youngsters cried; but the elders thought, "In prayer."

A boy threw stones; he picked them up and stored them in his vest;So tottered, muttered, mumbled he, till he died, perhaps found rest."Is there a reason in nature for these hard hearts?" O Lear,That a reason out of nature must turn them soft, seems clear!

Robert Browning.

GOOD KING WENCESLAS.

Good King Wenceslas looked out, On the feast of Stephen, When the snow lay round about, Deep, and crisp, and even; Brightly shone the moon that night, Tho' the frost was cruel, When a poor man came in sight, Gathering winter fuel.

"Hither, page, and stand by me, If thou know'st it, telling, Yonder peasant, who is he? Where and what his dwelling?" "Sire, he lives a good league hence, Underneath the mountain; Right against the forest fence, By Saint Agnes' fountain."

"Bring me flesh, and bring me wine, Bring me pine-logs hither: Thou and I will see him dine, When we bear them thither." Page and monarch forth they went, Forth they went together Thro' the rude wind's wild lament And the bitter weather.

"Sire, the night is darker now, And the wind blows stronger; Fails my heart, I know not how, I can go no longer." "Mark my footsteps, good my page; Tread thou in them boldly: Thou shalt find the winter's rage Freeze thy blood less coldly."

In his master's steps he trod, Where the snow lay dinted; Heat was in the very sod Which the saint had printed. Therefore, Christian men, be sure, Wealth or rank possessing, Ye who now will bless the poor, Shall yourselves find blessing.

Translated from the Latin, by J. M. Neale.

THE WISE MEN OF THE EAST.

Three kings went riding from the EastThrough fine weather and wet;"And whither shall we ride," they said,"Where we ha' not ridden yet?"

"And whither shall we ride," they said,"To find the hidden thingThat times the course of all our starsAnd all our auguring?"

They were the Wise Men of the East,And none so wise as they;"Alas!" the King of Persia cried,"And must ye ride away?

"Yet since ye go a-riding, sirs,I pray ye, ride for me,And carry me my golden giftsTo the King o' Galilee.

"Go riding into Palestine,A long ride and a fair!""'Tis well!" the Mages answered him,"As well as anywhere!"

They rode by day, they rode by night,The stars came out on high,—"And, oh!" said King Balthazar,As he gazed into the sky,

"We ride by day, we ride by night,To a King in Galilee;We leave a king in Persia,And kings no less are we.

"Yet often in the deep blue night,When stars burn far and dim,I wish I knew a greater King,To fall and worship him.

"A king who should not care to reign,But wonderful and fair;A king—a king that were a starAloft in miles of air!"

"A star is good," said Melchior,"A high, unworldly thing;But I would choose a soul aliveTo be my Lord and King.

"Not Herod, nay, nor Cyrus, nay,Not any king at all;For I would choose a new-born childLaid in a manger-stall."

"'Tis well," the black King Casper cried,"For mighty men are ye;But no such humble king were meetFor my simplicity.

"A star is small and very far,A babe's a simple thing;The very Son of God himselfShall be my Lord and King!"

Then smiled the King Balthazar;"A good youth!" Melchior cried;And young and old, without a word,Along the hills they ride,

Till, lo! among the western skiesThere grows a shining thing— "The star! Behold the star," they shout;"Behold Balthazar's King!"

And, lo! within the western skiesThe star begins to flit;The three kings spur their horses on,And follow after it.

And when they reach the king's palace,They cry, "Behold the place!"But, like a shining bird, the starFlits on in heaven apace.

Oh they rode on, and on they rode,Till they reached a lonely wold,Where shepherds keep their flocks by night,And the night was chill and cold.

Oh they rode on, and on they rode,Till they reach a little town,And there the star in heaven stands stillAbove a stable brown.

The town is hardly a village,The stable's old and poor,But there the star in heaven stands stillAbove the stable door.

And through the open door, the strawAnd the tired beasts they see;And the Babe, laid in a manger,That sleepeth peacefully.

"All hail, the King of Melchior!"The three Wise Men begin;King Melchior swings from off his horse,And he would have entered in.

But why do the horses whinny and neigh?And what thing fills the nightWith wheeling spires of angels,And streams of heavenly light?

Above the stable roof they turnAnd hover in a ring,And "Glory be to God on highAnd peace on earth," they sing.

King Melchior kneels upon the grassAnd falls a-praying there;Balthazar lets the bridle drop,And gazes in the air.

But Casper gives a happy shout,And hastens to the stall;"Now, hail!" he cries, "thou Son of God,And Saviour of us all."

A. Mary F. Robinson.

CHRISTMAS AT SEA.

The sheets were frozen hard, and they cut the naked hand; The decks were like a slide, where a seaman scarce could stand; The wind was a nor'wester, blowing squally off the sea; And cliffs and spouting breakers were the only things a-lee.

They heard the surf a-roaring before the break of day; But 'twas only with the peep of light we saw how ill we lay. We tumbled every hand on deck instanter, with a shout, And we gave her the maintops'l, and stood by to go about.

All day we tacked and tacked between the South Head and the North; All day we hauled the frozen sheets, and got no further forth; All day as cold as charity, in bitter pain and dread, For very life and nature, we tacked from head to head.

We gave the South a wider berth, for there the tide-race roared; But every tack we made we brought the North Head close aboard; So's we saw the cliffs and houses, and the breakers running high, And the coast-guard in his garden, with his glass against his eye.

The frost was on the village roofs as white as ocean foam; The good red fires were burning bright in every 'longshore home; The windows sparkled clear, and the chimneys volleyed out; And I vow we sniffed the victuals as the vessel went about.

The bells upon the church were rung with a mighty jovial cheer; For it's just that I should tell you how (of all days in the year) This day of our adversity was blessed Christmas morn, And the house above the coast-guard's was the house where I was born.

Oh, well I saw the pleasant room, the pleasant faces there, My mother's silver spectacles, my father's silver hair; And well I saw the firelight, like a flight of homely elves, Go dancing round the china plates that stand upon the shelves.

And well I knew the talk they had, the talk that was of me, Of the shadow on the household, and the son that went to sea; And, oh, the wicked fool I seemed, in every kind of way, To be here and hauling frozen ropes on blessed Christmas Day.

They lit the high sea-light, and the dark began to fall. "All hands to loose topgallant sails!" I heard the captain call. "By the Lord, she'll never stand it," our first mate, Jackson, cried.... "It's the one way or the other, Mr. Jackson," he replied.

She staggered to her bearings, but the sails were new and good, And the ship smelt up to windward just as though she understood. As the winter's day was ending, in the entry of the night, We cleared the weary headland, and passed below the light.

And they heaved a mighty breath, every soul on board but me, As they saw her nose again pointing handsome out to sea; But all that I could think of, in the darkness and the cold, Was just that I was leaving home and my folks were growing old.

Robert Louis Stevenson.

"LAST CHRISTMAS WAS A YEAR AGO."

(THE OLD LADY SPEAKS.)

Last Christmas was a year agoSays I to David, I-says-I,"We're goin' to mornin' service, soYou hitch up right away: I'll tryTo tell the girls jes what to doFer dinner. We'll be back by two."I didn't wait to hear what heWould more'n like say back to me,But banged the stable-door and flewBack to the house, jes plumb chilled through.

Cold! *Wooh!* how cold it was! My-oh!Frost *flyin'*, and the air, you know—"Jes sharp enough," heerd David swear,"To shave a man and cut his hair!"And blow *and* blow! and *snow* and snow,Where it had drifted 'long the fenceAnd 'crost the road,—some places, though,Jes swep' clean to the gravel, soThe goin' was as bad fer sleighsAs 't was fer wagons,—and *both* ways,'Twixt snow-drifts and the bare ground, I'veJes wondered we got through alive;I hain't saw nothin' 'fore er sence'At beat it *anywheres* I know—Last Christmas was a year ago.

And David said, as we set out,'At Christmas services was 'boutAs cold and wuthless kind o' loveTo offer up as *he* knowed of;And, as fer *him*, he railly thought'At the Good Bein' up aboveWould think more of us—as he ought—A-stayin' home on sich a dayAnd thankin' of him thataway.And jawed on in an undertone,'Bout leavin' Lide and Jane aloneThere on the place, and me not thereTo oversee 'em, and p'pareThe stuffin' for the turkey, andThe sass and all, you understand.

I've always managed David by Jes sayin' nothin'. That was why He'd chased Lide's beau away—'cause Lide She'd allus take up Perry's side When David tackled him; and so, Last Christmas was a year ago,—Er ruther 'bout a week afore,—David and Perry'd quarr'l'd about Some tom-fool argyment, you know, And pap told him to "Jes git out O' there, and not to come no more, And, when he went, to shet the door!" And as he passed the winder, we Saw Perry, white as white could be, March past, onhitch his hoss, and light A see-gyar, and lope out o' sight. Then Lide she come to me and cried. And I said nothin'—was no need. And yit, you know, that man jes got Right out o' there's ef he'd be'n shot—P'tendin' he must go and feed The stock er somepin'. Then I tried To git the pore girl pacified.

But gittin' back to—where was we?—Oh, yes—where David lectered me All way to meetin', high and low, Last Christmas was a year ago. Fer all the awful cold, they was A fair attendunce; mostly, though, The crowd was 'round the stoves, you see, Thawin' their heels and scrougin' us. Ef t'adn't be'n fer the old Squire Givin' his seat to us, as in We stompted, a-fairly perishin', And David could 'a' got no fire, He'd jes 'a' drapped there in his tracks. And Squire, as I was tryin' to yit Make room fer him, says, "No; the facks Is I got to git up and git 'Ithout no preachin'. Jes got word—Trial fer life—can't be deferred!" And out he put. And all way through The sermont—and a long one, too—I couldn't he'p but think o' Squire And us changed round so, and admire His gintle ways—to give his warm Bench up, and have to face the storm. And when I noticed David he Was needin' jabbin', I thought best To kind o' sort o' let him rest—'Peared like he slep' so peacefully! And then I thought o' home, and howAnd what the girls was doin' now,And kind o' prayed, 'way in my breast,And breshed away a tear er twoAs David waked, and church was through.

By time we'd "howdyed" round, and shuckHands with the neighbors, must 'a' tuckA half-hour longer: ever' oneA-sayin' "Christmas-gift!" aforeDavid er me—so we got none.But David warmed up, more and more,And got so jokey-like, and hadHis sperits up, and 'peared so glad,I whispered to him, "S'pose you astA passel of 'em come and eatTheir dinners with us.—Girls 's gotA full-and-plenty fer the lotAnd all their kin." So David passedThe invite round. And ever' seatIn ever' wagon-bed and sleighWas jes *packed*, as we rode away—The young folks, mild er so along,A-strikin' up a sleighin' song.Tel David laughed and yelled, you know,And jes whirped up and sent the snowAnd gravel flyin' thick and fast—Last Christmas was a year ago.W'y, that-air seven-mild ja'nt we come—Jes seven mild scant from church to home—It didn't 'pear, that day, to beMuch furder railly 'n 'bout three.

But I was purty squeamish byThe time home hove in sight and ISee two vehickles standin' thereAlready. So says I, "Prepare!"All to myse'f. And presentlyDavid he sobered; and says he,"Hain't that-air Squire Hanch's oldBuggy," he says, "and claybank mare?"Says I, "Le's git in out the cold—Your company's nigh 'bout froze." He says,"Whose sleigh's that-air a-standin' there?"Says I, "It's no odds whose—you jesDrive to the house and let us out,'Cause we're jes freezin', nigh about."Well, David swung up to the doorAnd out we piled. At first I heerdJane's voice; then *Lide's*—I thought aforeI reached that girl I'd jes die,

shore;And when I reached her, wouldn't keeredMuch ef I had, I was
so glad,A-kissin' her through my green veil,And jes excitin' her so
bad'At she broke down, herse'f—and JaneShe cried—and we all
hugged again.And David—David jes turned pale!—Looked at the
girls and then at me,Then at the open door—and then"Is old
Squire Hanch in there?" says he.The old Squire suddently stood
inThe doorway, with a sneakin' grin."Is Perry Anders in there,
too?"Says David, limberin' all through,As Lide and me both
grabbed him, andPerry stepped out and waved his handAnd says,
"Yes, pap." And David jes.Stooped and kissed Lide, and says, "I
guessYour mother's much to blame as you.Ef she kin resk him, I
kin too."

The dinner we had then hain't noBit better'n the one to-day'At
we'll have fer 'em. Hear some sleighA-jinglin' now.—David,
fer me,I wish you'd jes go out and seeEf they're in sight yit. It jes
doesMe good to think, in times like these,Lide's done so well. And
David he'sMore tractabler 'n what he wasLast Christmas was a
year ago.

James Whitcomb Riley.

As It Fell Upon A Day.

"A handsome hostess, merry host, A pot of ale and now a toast, Tobacco, and a good coal-fire, Are things this season doth require."

Poor Robin.

Ready for the Feast

A CHRISTMAS "NOW."

So, now is come our joyful'st feast, Let every man be jolly; Each room with ivy-leaves is drest, And every post with holly. Though some churls at our mirth repine, Round your foreheads garlands twine; Drown sorrow in a cup of wine, And let us all be merry.

Now all our neighbors' chimneys smoke, And Christmas logs are burning; Their ovens they with baked meats choke, And all their spits are turning. Without the door let sorrow lie; And if for cold it hap to die, We'll bury 't in a Christmas-pie, And evermore be merry.

Now every lad is wondrous trim, And no man minds his labor; Our lasses have provided them A bagpipe and a tabor; Young men and maids, and girls and boys, Give life to one another's joys; And you anon shall by their noise Perceive that they are merry.

Rank misers now do sparing shun; Their hall of music soundeth; And dogs thence with whole shoulders run, So all things there aboundeth. The country folks themselves advance For crowdy-mutton's come out of France; And Jack shall pipe, and Jill shall dance, And all the town be merry.

Ned Squash has fetched his bands from pawn, And all his best apparel; Brisk Ned hath bought a ruff of lawn With droppings of the barrel; And those that hardly all the year Had bread to eat or rags to wear Will have both clothes and dainty fare, And all the day be merry.

Now poor men to the justicesWith capons make their arrants;And if they hap to fail of these,They plague them with their warrants:But now they feed them with good cheer,And what they want they take in beer;For Christmas comes but once a year,And then they shall be merry.

Good farmers in the country nurseThe poor that else were undone;Some landlords spend their money worseOn lust and pride at London.There the roysters they do play,Drab and dice their lands away,Which may be ours another day;And therefore let's be merry.

The client now his suit forbears,The prisoner's heart is eased;The debtor drinks away his cares,And for the time is pleased.Though other purses be more fat,Why should we pine or grieve at that?Hang sorrow! care will kill a cat,And therefore let's be merry.

Hark! how the wags abroad do callEach other forth to rambling:Anon you'll see them in the hallFor nuts and apples scrambling.Hark! how the roofs with laughter sound!Anon they'll think the house goes round:For they the cellar's depth have found,And there they will be merry.

The wenches with their wassail bowls,About the streets are singing;The boys are come to catch the owls,The wild mare in is bringing.Our kitchen-boy hath broke his box,And to the dealing of the oxOur honest neighbors come by flocks,And here they will be merry.

Now kings and queens poor sheep-cotes have,And mate with everybody;The honest now may play the knave,And wise men play at noddy. Some youths will now a mumming go, Some others play at Rowland-ho, And twenty other gameboys mo, Because they will be merry.

Then wherefore in these merry days, Should we, I pray, be duller? No, let us sing some roundelays To make our mirth the fuller. And, whilst thus inspired, we sing, Let all the streets with echoes ring, Woods, and hills, and everything Bear witness we are merry.

George Wither.

CHRISTMAS EVE CUSTOMS.

I.

Come, guard this night the Christmas-pie,That the thief, though ne'er so sly,With his flesh-hooks, don't come nighTo catch it,

From him, who alone sits there,Having his eyes still in his ear,And a deal of nightly fearTo watch it!

II.

Wash your hands, or else the fireWill not teend[D] to your desire;Unwashed hands, ye maidens, know,Dead the fire, though ye blow.

Robert Herrick.

FOOTNOTE:

[D] Burn.

MERRY SOULS.

O you merry, merry Souls, Christmas is a-coming, We shall have flowing bowls, Dancing, piping, drumming.

Delicate minced pies To feast every virgin, Capon and goose likewise, Brawn and a dish of sturgeon.

Then, for your Christmas box, Sweet plum-cakes and money, Delicate Holland smocks, Kisses sweet as honey.

Hey for the Christmas ball, Where we shall be jolly Jigging short and tall, Kate, Dick, Ralph, and Molly.

Then to the hop we'll go Where we'll jig and caper; Maidens all-a-row; Will shall pay the scraper.

Hodge shall dance with Prue, Keeping time with kisses; We'll have a jovial crew Of sweet smirking misses.

Round About Our Coal Fire.

The Baron's Hall

CHRISTMAS IN THE OLDEN TIME.

The damsel donned her kirtle sheen;The hall was dressed with holly green;Forth to the wood did merry-men goTo gather in the mistletoe.Then opened wide the baron's hallTo vassal, tenant, serf, and all;Power laid his rod of rule aside,And ceremony doffed his pride.The heir, with roses in his shoes,That night might village partner choose;The lord underogating shareThe vulgar game of post-and-pair.All hailed with uncontrolled delightAnd general voice, the happy night, That to the cottage as the crownBrought tidings of salvation down.The fire with well-dried logs suppliedWent roaring up the chimney wide;The huge hall-table's oaken face,Scrubbed till it shone, the day to grace,Bore then upon its massive boardNo mark to part the squire and lord.Then was brought in the lusty brawnBy old blue-coated serving-man;Then the grim boar's head frowned on high,Crested with bay and rosemary.Well can the green-garbed ranger tellHow, when, and where the monster fell;What dogs before his death he tore,And all the baiting of the boar.The wassail round, in good brown bowls,Garnished with ribbons blithely trowls.There the huge sirloin reeked; hard byPlum-porridge stood and Christmas-pie;Nor failed old Scotland to produceAt such high tide her savory goose.Then came the merry masquers inAnd carols roared with blithesome din;If unmelodious was the song,It was a hearty note and strong.Who lists may in their mumming seeTraces of ancient mystery.While shirts supplied the masquerade,And smutted cheeks the visors made:But, oh! what masquers richly dightCan boast of bosoms half so light!England was merry England whenOld Christmas brought his sports again.'Twas Christmas broached the mightiest ale,'Twas Christmas told the merriest tale;A Christmas gambol oft would cheerThe poor man's heart through half the year.

Sir Walter Scott.

CEREMONIES FOR CHRISTMAS.

Come, bring with a noise, My merry, merry boys, The Christmas-log to the firing, While my good dame, she Bids ye all be free, And drink to your heart's desiring.

With the last year's brand Light the new block, and, For good success in his spending, On your psalteries play, That sweet luck may Come while the log is a-teending. [E]

Drink now the strong beer, Cut the white loaf here, The while the meat is a-shredding; For the rare mince-pie And the plums stand by, To fill the paste that's a-kneading.

Robert Herrick.

FOOTNOTE:

[E] Burning.

BRINGING IN THE BOAR'S HEAD.

*Caput apri deferoReddens laudes domino.*The boar's head in hand bring I,With garlands gay and rosemary;I pray you all sing merrily*Qui estis in convivio.*

The boar's head, I understand,Is the chief service in this land;Look, wherever it be fand,.*Servite cum cantico.*

Be glad, lords, both more and less,For this hath ordained our stewardTo cheer you all this Christmas,The boar's head with mustard.

Ritson's Ancient Songs.

THE BOAR'S HEAD CAROL.

SUNG AT QUEEN'S COLLEGE, OXFORD.

The boar's head in hand bear I,Bedecked with bays and rosemary;And I pray you, my masters, be merry,Quot estis in convivio.Caput apri deferoReddens laudes domino.

The boar's head, as I understand,Is the rarest dish in all this land,Which thus bedeck'd with a gay garlandLet us servire cantico.Caput apri deferoReddens laudes domino.

Our steward hath provided thisIn honor of the King of bliss;Which on this day to be served isIn Reginensi Atrio.Caput apri deferoReddens laudes domino.

TO BE EATEN WITH MUSTARD.

SUNG AT ST. JOHN'S COLLEGE, OXFORD, CHRISTMAS, 1607.

The boar is dead, So, here is his head; What man could have done moreThan his head off to strike, Meleager-like, And bring it as I do before.

He living spoiledWhere good men toiled, Which made kind Ceres sorry; But now dead and drawnIs very good brawn, And we have brought it for ye.

Then set down the swineyard, The foe to the vineyard, Let Bacchus crown his fall; Let this boar's head and mustardStand for pig, goose, and custard, And so ye are welcome all.

CHRISTMAS DAY IN THE MORNING.

Maids, get up and bake your pies, Bake your pies, bake your pies; Maids, get up and bake your pies, 'Tis Christmas day in the morning.

See the ships all sailing by, Sailing by, sailing by; See the ships all sailing by On Christmas day in the morning.

Dame, what made your ducks to die, Ducks to die, ducks to die; Dame, what made your ducks to die On Christmas day in the morning?

You let your lazy maidens lie, Maidens lie, maidens lie; You let your lazy maidens lie On Christmas day in the morning.

Bishoprick Garland, a.d. 1834.

PRAISE OF CHRISTMAS.

FIRST PART.

All hail to the days that merit more praiseThan all the rest of the year,And welcome the nights that double delightsAs well for the poor as the peer!Good fortune attend each merry-man's friend,That doth but the best that he may;Forgetting old wrongs, with carols and songs,To drive the cold winter away.

Let Misery pack, with a whip at his back,To the deep Tantalian flood;In Lethe profound let envy be drown'd,That pines at another man's good;Let Sorrow's expense be banded from hence,All payments have greater delay,We'll spend the long nights in cheerful delightsTo drive the cold winter away.

'Tis ill for a mind to anger inclinedTo think of small injuries now;If wrath be to seek, do not lend her thy cheek,Nor let her inhabit thy brow,Cross out of thy books malevolent looks,Both beauty and youth's decay,And wholly consort with mirth and with sportTo drive the cold winter away.

The court in all state now opens her gateAnd gives a free welcome to most;The city likewise, tho' somewhat precise,Doth willingly part with her roast:But yet by report from city and courtThe country will e'er gain the day;More liquor is spent and with better contentTo drive the cold winter away.

Our good gentry there for costs do not spare,The yeomanry fast not till Lent;The farmers and such think nothing too much,If they keep but to pay for their rent.The poorest of all now do merrily call, When at a fit place they can stay, For a song or a tale or a cup of good aleTo drive the cold winter away.

Thus none will allow of solitude nowBut merrily greets the time, To make it appear of all the whole yearThat this is accounted the prime:December is seen apparell'd in green, And January fresh as MayComes dancing along with a cup and a songTo drive the cold winter away.

SECOND PART.

This time of the year is spent in good cheer,And neighbors together do meetTo sit by the fire, with friendly desire,Each other in love to greet;Old grudges forgot are put in the pot,All sorrows aside they lay;The old and the young doth carol this songTo drive the cold winter away.

Sisley and Nanny, more jocund than any,As blithe as the month of June,Do carol and sing like birds of the spring,No nightingale sweeter in tune;To bring in content, when summer is spent,In pleasant delight and play,With mirth and good cheer to end the whole year,And drive the cold winter away.

The shepherd, the swain, do highly disdainTo waste out their time in care;And Clim of the Clough hath plenty enoughIf he but a penny can spareTo spend at the night, in joy and delight,Now after his labor all day;For better than lands is the help of his handsTo drive the cold winter away.

To mask and to mum kind neighbors will comeWith wassails of nut-brown ale,To drink and carouse to all in the houseAs merry as bucks in the dale;Where cake, bread, and cheese are brought for your feesTo make you the longer stay;At the fire to warm 'twill do you no harm,To drive the cold winter away.

When Christmas's tide comes in like a brideWith holly and ivy clad,Twelve days in the year much mirth and good cheerIn every household is had;The country guise is then to deviseSome gambols of Christmas play,Whereat the young men do best that they canTo drive the cold winter away.

When white-bearded frost hath threatened his worst, And fallen from branch and brier, Then time away calls from husbandry halls And from the good countryman's fire, Together to go to plough and to sow, To get us both food and array, And thus with content the time we have spent To drive the cold winter away.

WINTER'S DELIGHTS.

Now winter nights enlargeThe number of their hours,And clouds their storms dischargeUpon the airy towers.Let now the chimneys blaze,And cups o'erflow with wine;Let well-tuned words amazeWith harmony divine.Now yellow waxen lightsShall wait on honey love,While youthful revels, masques, and courtly sightsSleep's leaden spells remove.

The time doth well dispenseWith lovers' long discourse;Much speech hath some defence,Though beauty no remorse.All do not all things well:Some, measures comely tread,Some, knotted riddles tell,Some, poems smoothly read.The summer hath his joys,And winter his delights;Though love and all his pleasures are but toys,They shorten tedious nights.

Thomas Campion.

A CHRISTMAS CATCH.

To shorten winter's sadness,See where the nymphs with gladnessDisguised all are coming,Right wantonly a-mumming.Fa la.

Whilst youthful sports are lasting,To feasting turn our fasting;With revels and with wassailsMake grief and care our vassals.Fa la.

For youth it well beseemethThat pleasure he esteemeth;And sullen age is hatedThat mirth would have abated.Fa la.

Thomas Weelkes, a.d. 1597.

THE EPIC.

At Francis Allen's on the Christmas eve,—The game of forfeits done—the girls all kissedBeneath the sacred bush and past away,—The parson Holmes, the poet Everard Hall,The host, and I sat round the wassail-bowl,Then half-way ebbed: and there we held a talk,How all the old honor had from Christmas gone,Or gone, or dwindled down to some odd gamesIn some odd nooks like this; till I, tired outWith cutting eights that day upon the pond,Where, three times slipping from the outer edge,I bumped the ice into three several stars,Fell in a doze; and, half-awake, I heardThe parson taking wide and wider sweeps,Now harping on the church-commissioners,Now hawking at geology and schism;Until I woke, and found him settled downUpon the general decay of faithRight through the world; "at home was little left,And none abroad; there was no anchor, none,To hold by." Francis, laughing, clapt his handOn Everard's shoulder with, "I hold by him.""And I," quoth Everard, "by the wassail-bowl.""Why, yes," I said, "we knew your gift that wayAt college; but another which you had,I mean of verse (for so we held it then),What came of that?" "You know," said Frank, "he burntHis epic, his King Arthur, some twelve books,"—And then to me demanding why? "Oh, sir,He thought that nothing new was said, or elseSomething so said 'twas nothing—that a truthLooks freshest in the fashion of the day:God knows, he has a mint of reasons: ask.It pleased me well enough." "Nay, nay," said Hall,"Why take the style of those heroic times?For nature brings not back the mastodon,Nor we those times; and why should any manRemodel models? These twelve

---

59

books of mineWere faint Homeric echoes, nothing-worth,Mere chaff and draff, much better burnt." "But I,"Said Francis, "picked the eleventh from this hearth,And have it: keep a thing, its use will come.I hoard it as a sugar-plum for Holmes."He laughed, and I, though sleepy, like a horseThat hears the corn-bin open, pricked my ears;For I remembered Everard's college fameWhen we were freshmen: then, at my request,He brought it; and the poet, little urged,But, with some prelude of disparagement,Read, mouthing out his hollow oes and aes,Deep-chested music, and to this result:

MORTE D'ARTHUR.

So all day long the noise of battle rolledAmong the mountains by the winter sea;Until King Arthur's table, man by man,Had fallen in Lyonesse about their Lord,King Arthur: then, because his wound was deep,The bold Sir Bedivere uplifted him,Sir Bedivere, the last of all his knights,And bore him to a chapel nigh the field,A broken chancel with a broken cross,That stood on a dark strait of barren land.On one side lay the ocean, and on oneLay a great water, and the moon was full.Then spake King Arthur to Sir Bedivere:"The sequel of to-day unsolders allThe goodliest fellowship of famous knightsWhereof this world holds record. Such a sleepThey sleep—the men I loved. I think that weShall nevermore, at any future time,Delight our souls with talk of knightly deeds,Walking about the gardens and the hallsOf Camelot, as in the days that were.I perish by this people which I made,—Tho' Merlin sware that I should come againTo rule once more,—but let what will be, be,I am so deeply smitten thro' the helmThat without help I cannot last till morn.Thou, therefore, take my brand, Excalibur,Which was my pride: for thou rememberest howIn those old days, one summer noon, an armRose up from out the bosom of the lake,Clothed in white samite, mystic, wonderful,Holding the sword—and how I rowed acrossAnd took it, and have worn it, like a king:And, whensoever I am sung or toldIn after time, this also shall be known:But now delay not: take ExcaliburAnd fling him far into the middle mere:Watch what thou seest, and lightly bring me word."To him replied the bold Sir Bedivere:"It is not meet, Sir King, to leave thee thus,Aidless, alone, and smitten through the helm.A little thing may harm a wounded man,Yet I thy hest will all perform at full,Watch what I see, and lightly bring thee word."So saying, from the ruined shrine he steptAnd in the moon athwart the place of tombs,Where lay the mighty bones of ancient men,Old knights, and over them the sea-wind sang.Shrill, chill, with flakes of foam. He, stepping downBy zigzag paths and juts of pointed rock,Came on the shining levels of the lake.There drew he forth the brand Excalibur,And o'er him, drawing it, the winter moonBrightening the skirts of a long cloud, ran forthAnd sparkled keen with frost against the hilt:For all the haft twinkled with diamond sparks,Myriads of topaz-lights and jacinth-workOf subtlest jewelry. He gazed so longThat both his eyes were dazzled, as he stood,This way and that dividing the swift mind,In act to throw: but at the last it seemedBetter to leave Excalibur concealedThere in the many-knotted water-flagsThat whistled stiff and dry about the marge.So strode he back slow to the wounded King.Then spake King Arthur to Sir Bedivere:"Hast thou performed my mission which I gave?What is it thou hast seen? or what hast heard?"And answer made the bold Sir Bedivere:"I heard the ripple washing in the reeds,And the wild water lapping on the crag."To whom replied King Arthur, faint and pale:"Thou hast betrayed thy nature and thy name,Not rendering true answer, as beseemedThy fealty, nor like a noble knight:For surer sign had followed, either hand,Or voice, or else a motion of the mere.This is a shameful thing for men to lie.Yet now, I charge thee, quickly go againAs thou art lief and dear, and do the thingI bad thee, watch, and lightly bring me word."Then went Sir Bedivere the second timeAcross the ridge and paced beside the mere,Counting the dewy pebbles, fixed in thought;But when he saw the wonder of the hilt,How curiously and strangely chased, he smoteHis palms together, and he cried aloud,"And if, indeed, I cast the brand away,Surely a precious thing, one worthy note,Should thus be lost forever from the earth,Which might have pleased the eyes of many men.What good should follow this, if this were done?What harm, undone? deep harm to disobey,Seeing obedience is the bond of rule.Were it well to obey then, if a king demandAn act unprofitable against himself?"

*   *   *   *   *

So spake he, clouded with his own conceit,And hid Excalibur the second time,And so strode back slow to the wounded King.Then spoke King Arthur, breathing heavily:"What is it thou hast seen? or what hast heard?"And answer made the bold Sir Bedivere:"I heard the water lapping on the crag,And the long ripple washing in the reeds."To whom replied King Arthur much in wrath:"Ah, miserable and unkind, untrue,Unknightly, traitor-hearted! Woe is me!Authority forgets a dying king,Laid widowed of the power of his eyeThat bowed the will. I see thee what thou art;For thou, the latest left of all my knights,In whom should meet the offices of all,Thou wouldst betray me for the precious hilt;Either from lust of gold, or like a girlValuing the giddy pleasure of the eyes.Yet, for a man may fail in duty twice,And the third time may prosper, get thee hence;But, if thou spare to fling Excalibur,I will arise and slay thee with my hands."Then quickly rose Sir Bedivere and ran,And, leaping down the ridges lightly, plungedAmong the bulrush-beds, and clutched the swordAnd strongly wheeled and threw it. The great brandMade lightnings in the splendor of the moon,And flashing round and round, and whirled in an arch,Shot like a streamer of the northern morn,Seen where the moving isles of winter shockBy night, with noises of the northern sea,So flashed and fell the brand Excalibur:But ere he dipt the surface, rose an armClothed in white samite, mystic, wonderful,And caught him by the hilt and brandished himThree times, and drew him under in the mere.And lightly went the other to the King.

* * * * *

Here ended Hall, and our last light, that longHad winked, and threatened darkness, flared and fell:At which the Parson, sent to sleep with sound,And waked with silence, grunted "Good!" but weSat rapt: it was the tone with which he read—Perhaps some modern touches here and thereRedeemed it from the charge of nothingness—Or else we loved the man, and prized his work;I know not; but we sitting as I said,The cock crew loud; as at that time of yearThe lusty bird takes every hour for dawn:Then Francis, muttering, like a man ill-used,"There now—that's nothing!" drew a little back,And drove his heel into the smouldered log,That sent a blast of sparkles up the flue:And so to bed; where yet in sleep I seemedTo sail with Arthur under looming shores,Point after point; till on to dawn, when dreamsBegin to feel the truth and stir of day,To me, methought, who waited with a crowd,Then came a bark that, blowing forward, bore]King Arthur, like a modern gentlemanOf stateliest port; and all the people cried,"Arthur is come again: he cannot die."Then those that stood upon the hills behindRepeated "Come again, and thrice as fair;"And, further inland, voices echoed, "ComeWith all good things, and war shall be no more."At this a hundred bells began to peal,That with the sound I woke, and heard indeedThe clear church-bells ring in the Christmas morn.

Lord Tennyson.

THE COUNTRY LIFE.

For sports, for pageantries, and plays,Thou hast thy eves and holidaysOn which the young men and maids meetTo exercise their dancing feet,Tripping the comely country-round,With daffodils and daisies crowned.Thy wakes, thy quintals, here thou hast,Thy May-poles, too, with garlands graced,Thy morris-dance, thy Whitsun-ale,Thy shearing-feast, which never fail,Thy harvest home, thy wassail-bowl,That's tossed up after fox-i'-th'-hole,Thy mummeries, thy Twelfthtide kingsAnd queens, thy Christmas revellings,Thy nut-brown mirth, thy russet wit,And no man pays too dear for it.

O happy life! if that their goodThe husbandmen but understood,Who all the day themselves do pleaseAnd younglings with such sports as these,And, lying down, have naught t' affrightSweet sleep, that makes more short the night.

Robert Herrick.

CHRISTMAS OMNIPRESENT.

Christmas comes! He comes, he comes,Ushered with a rain of plums;Hollies in the windows greet him;Schools come driving post to meet him;Gifts precede him, bells proclaim him,Every mouth delights to name him;Wet, and cold, and wind, and darkMake him but the warmer mark;And yet he comes not one-embodied,Universal's the blithe godhead,And in every festal housePresence hath ubiquitous.Curtains, those snug room-enfolders,Hang upon his million shoulders,And he has a million eyesOf fire, and eats a million pies,And is very merry and wise;Very wise and very merry,And loves a kiss beneath the berry.Then full many a shape hath he,All in said ubiquity:Now is he a green array,And now an "eve," and now a "day;"Now he's town gone out of town,And now a feast in civic gown,And now the pantomime and clownWith a crack upon the crown,And all sorts of tumbles down;And then he's music in the night,And the money gotten by't:He's a man that can't write verses,Bringing some to ope your purses:He's a turkey, he's a goose,He's oranges unfit for use;He's a kiss that loves to growUnderneath the mistletoe;And he's forfeits, cards, and wassails,And a king and queen with vassals,All the "quizzes" of the timeDrawn and quarter'd with a rhyme;And then, for their revival's sake,Lo! he's an enormous cake,With a sugar on the top,Seen before in many a shop,Where the boys could gaze forever,They think the cake so very clever.Then, some morning, in the lurchLeaving romps, he goes to church,Looking very grave and thankful,After which he's just as prankful.Now a saint, and now a sinner,But, above all, he's a dinner;He's a dinner, where you seeEverybody's family;Beef, and pudding, and mince-pies,And little boys with laughing eyes,Whom their seniors ask arch questions,Feigning fears of indigestionsAs if they, forsooth, the old ones,Hadn't, privately, tenfold ones:He's a dinner and a fire,Heap'd beyond your heart's desire,—Heap'd with log, and bak'd with coals,Till it roasts your very souls,And your cheek the fire outstares,And you all push back your chairs,And the mirth becomes too great,And you all sit up too late,Nodding all with too much head,And so go off to too much bed.

O plethora of beef and bliss!Monkish feaster, sly of kiss!Southern soul in body Dutch!Glorious time of great Too-Much!Too much heat and too much noise,Too much babblement of boys;Too much eating, too much drinking,Too much ev'rything but thinking;Solely bent to laugh and stuff,And trample upon base Enough.Oh, right is thy instructive praiseOf the wealth of Nature's ways!Right thy most unthrifty glee,And pious thy mince-piety!For, behold! great Nature's selfBuilds her no abstemious shelf,But provides (her love is suchFor all) her own great, good Too-Much,—Too much grass, and too much tree,Too much air, and land, and sea,Too much seed of fruit and flower,And fish, an unimagin'd dower!(In whose single roe shall beLife enough to stock the sea,—Endless ichthyophagy!)Ev'ry instant through the dayWorlds of life are thrown away;Worlds of life, and worlds of pleasure,Not for lavishment of treasure,But because she's so immenselyRich, and loves us so intensely.She would have us, once for all,Wake at her benignant call,And all grow wise, and all lay downStrife, and jealousy, and frown,And, like the sons of one great mother, Share, and be blest, with one another.

Leigh Hunt.

AN OLD ENGLISH CHRISTMAS-TIDE.

Thrice holy ring, afar and wide, The merry bells this Christmas-tide; Afar and wide, through hushed snow, From ivied minster-portico, Sweet anthems swell to tell the tale Of that young babe the shepherds hail Sitting amid their nibbling flocks What time the Hallelujah shocks The drowsy earth, and Cherubim Break through the heaven with harp and hymn.

Belated birds sing tingling notes To warm apace their chilly throats, Or they, mayhap, have caught the story And pipe their part from branches hoary; While up aloft, his tempered beams The sun has poured in gentle streams, Sending o'er snowy hill and dell A pleasance to greet the Christmas bell! Now every yeoman starts abroad For holly green and the ivy-tod; Good folk to kirk are soon atrip Mellow with cheer and good-fellowship, And cosey chimneys, here and there Puff forth the sweets o' Christmas fare.

Ho! rosy wenches and merry men From over the hill and field and fen, Great store is here, the drifts between Of myrtle red-berried, and mistletoe green! Ho, Phyllis and Kate and bonny Nell Come hither, and buffet the goodmen well, An they gather not for *hall* and hearth, Fair bays to grace the evening mirth. Aye, laugh ye well! and echoed wide Your voices sing through the Christmas-tide, And wintry winds emblend their tones At the minster-eaves with the organ groans: The carols meet with laughter sweet In a gay embrace mid the drifting sleet.

Anon the weary sun's at rest, And clouds that hovered all day by, Like silver arras down the sky Enfold him—while the winds are whist—But not the Christmas jollity,For, little space, and wassail highFlows at the board; and hautboys soundThe tripping dance and merry round.Here youths and maidens stand in rowKissing beneath the mistletoe;And many a tale of midnight routO' Christmas-tide the woods about,Of faery meetings beneath the moonIn wintry blast or summer swoon,Goes round the hearth, while all aglowThe yule-log crackles the crane below.

Drink hael! good folk, by the chimney side,O sweet's the holy Christmas-tide!Drink hael! Drink hael! and pledge again:"Here's peace on earth, good-will to men!"

H. S. M.

SIGNS OF CHRISTMAS.

When on the barn's thatch'd roof is seenThe moss in tufts of liveliest green;When Roger to the wood pile goes,And, as he turns, his fingers blows;When all around is cold and drear,Be sure that Christmas-tide is near.

When up the garden walk in vainWe seek for Flora's lovely train;When the sweet hawthorn bower is bare,And bleak and cheerless is the air;When all seems desolate around,Christmas advances o'er the ground.

When Tom at eve comes home from plough,And brings the mistletoe's green bough,With milk-white berries spotted o'er,And shakes it the sly maids before,Then hangs the trophy up on high,Be sure that Christmas-tide is nigh.

When Hal, the woodman, in his clogs,Bears home the huge unwieldly logs,That, hissing on the smould'ring fire,Flame out at last a quiv'ring spire;When in his hat the holly stands,Old Christmas musters up his bands.

When cluster'd round the fire at night,Old William talks of ghost and sprite,And, as a distant out-house gateSlams by the wind, they fearful wait,While some each shadowy nook explore,Then Christmas pauses at the door.

When Dick comes shiv'ring from the yard,And says the pond is frozen hard,While from his hat, all white with snow,The moisture, trickling, drops below,While carols sound, the night to cheer,Then Christmas and his train are here.

Edwin Lees.

THE MISTLETOE.

When winter nights grow long,And winds without blow cold,We sit in a ring round the warm wood-fire,And listen to stories old!And we try to look grave, (as maids should be,)When the men bring in boughs of the Laurel-tree.O the Laurel, the evergreen tree!The poets have laurels, and why not we?

How pleasant, when night falls downAnd hides the wintry sun,To see them come in to the blazing fire,And know that their work is done;Whilst many bring in, with a laugh or rhyme,Green branches of Holly for Christmas time!O the Holly, the bright green Holly,It tells (like a tongue) that the times are jolly!

Sometimes— (in our grave house,Observe, this happeneth not;)But, at times, the evergreen laurel boughsAnd the holly are all forgot!And then! what then? why, the men laugh lowAnd hang up a branch of the Mistletoe!O brave is the Laurel! and brave is the Holly!But the Mistletoe banisheth melancholy!Ah, nobody knows, nor ever shall know,What is done—under the Mistletoe.

Bryan Waller Proctor.

CHRISTMAS OF OLD.

IN GERMANY.

Three weeks before the day whereon was born the Lord of grace,And on the Thursday, boys and girls do run in every place,And bounce and beat at every door, with blows and lusty snaps,And cry the advent of the Lord, not born as yet, perhaps:And wishing to the neighbors all, that in the houses dwell,A happy year, and everything to spring and prosper well:Here have they pears, and plums, and pence; each man gives willingly,For these three nights are always thought unfortunate to be,Wherein they are afraid of sprites and cankered witches' spite,And dreadful devils, black and grim, that then have chiefest might.

In these same days, young, wanton girls that meet for marriage be,Do search to know the names of them that shall their husbands be.Four onions, five, or eight they take, and make in every oneSuch names as they do fancy most and best do think upon.Thus near the chimney then they set, and that same onion thanThe first doth sprout doth surely bear the name of their good man.Their husband's nature eke they seek to know and all his guise:When as the sun hath hid himself, and left the starry skies,Unto some woodstack do they go, and while they there do stand,Each one draws out a fagot stick, the next that comes to hand,Which if it straight and even be, and have no knots at all,A gentle husband then they think shall surely to them fall;But, if it foul and crooked be, and knotty here and there,A crabbed, churlish husband then they earnestly do fear.

Then comes the day wherein the Lord did bring his birth to pass, Whereas at midnight up they rise, and every man to Mass. This time so holy counted is, that divers earnestly Do think the waters all to wine are changèd suddenly In that same hour that Christ himself was born and came to light, And unto water straight again transformed and altered quite. There are beside that mindfully the money still do watch That first to altar comes, which then they privily do snatch. The priests, lest other should it have, take oft the same away, Whereby they think throughout the year to have good luck in play, And not to lose: then straight at game till daylight do they strive To make some present proof how well their hallowed pence will thrive.

This done, a wooden child in clouts is on the altar set, About the which both boys and girls do dance and trimly get, And carols sing in praise of Christ, and for to help them here The organs answer every verse with sweet and solemn cheer. The priests do roar aloud, and round about the parents stand, To see the sport, and with their voice do help them and their hand. Thus wont the Coribants perhaps upon the mountain Ide, The crying noise of Jupiter, new born, with song to hide, To dance about him round, and on their brazen pans to beat, Lest that his father, finding him, should him destroy and eat.

Then followeth Saint Stephen's Day, whereon doth every man His horses jaunt and course abroad, as swiftly as he can. Until they do extremely sweat, and then they let them blood, For this being done upon this day, they say doth do them good, And keeps them from all maladies and sickness through the year, As if that Stephen any time took charge of horses here. Next, John, the son of Zebedee, hath his appointed day,Who once, by cruel tyrant's will, constrained was, they say,Strong poison up to drink, therefore the Papists do believeThat whoso puts their trust in him, no poison them can grieve.The wine beside that hallowed is, in worship of his name,The priests do give the people that bring money for the same.And after with the selfsame wine are little manchets[F] made,Against the boisterous winter storms, and sundry such like trade.The men upon this solemn day do take this holy wine,To make them strong, so do the maids to make them fair and fine.

Then comes the day that calls to mind the cruel Herod's strife,Who seeking Christ to kill, the King of everlasting life,Destroyèd all the infants young, a beast unmerciless,And put to death all such as were of two years age or less.To them the sinful wretches cry and earnestly do prayTo get them pardon for their faults, and wipe their sins away.The parents, when this day appears, do beat their children allThough nothing they deserve, and servants all to beating fall,And monks do whip each other well, or else their Prior great,Or Abbot mad, doth take in hand their breeches all to beatIn worship of these Innocents, or rather, as we see,In honor of the cursèd king that did this cruelty.

The next to this is New-Year's Day, whereon to every friendThey costly presents in do bring and New-Year's gifts do send.These gifts the husband gives his wife, and father eke the child,And master on his men bestows the like, with favor mild,And good beginning of the year they wish and wish again,According to the ancient guise of heathen people vain.These eight days no man doth require his debts of any man,Their tables do they furnish out with all the meat they can:With marchpanes, tarts, and custards great they drink with staring eyes,They rout and revel, feed and feast as merry all as pies,As if they should at the entrance of this New Year have to die,Yet would they have their bellies full and ancient friends ally.

The Wise Men's day here followeth, who out from Persia far,Brought gifts and presents unto Christ, conducted by a star.The Papists do believe that these were kings, and so them call,And do affirm that of the same there were but three in all.Here sundry friends together come, and meet in company,And make a king amongst themselves by voice or destiny;Who, after princely guise, appoints his officers alway,Then unto feasting do they go, and long time after play:Upon their boards, in order thick, their dainty dishes stand,Till that their purses empty be and creditors at hand.Their children herein follow them, and choosing princes here,With pomp and great solemnity, they meet and make good cheerWith money either got by stealth, or of their parents eft,That so they may be trained to know both riot here and theft.Then, also, every householder, to his ability,Doth make a mighty cake that may suffice his company:Herein a penny doth he put, before it comes to fire,This he divides according as his household doth require;And every piece distributeth, as round about they stand,Which in their names unto the poor is given out of hand.But whoso chanceth on the piece wherein the money liesIs counted king amongst them all, and is with shouts and criesExalted to the heavens up, who, taking chalk in hand,Doth make a cross on every beam and rafters as they stand:Great force and power have these against all injuries and harms,Of cursed devils, sprites and bugs, of conjurings and charms,So much this king can do, so much the crosses bring to pass,Made by some servant, maid or child, or by some foolish ass!

Twice six nights then from Christmas they do count with diligence,Wherein each master in his house doth burn up frankincense:And on the table sets a loaf, when night approacheth near,Before the coals and frankincense to be perfumed there:First bowing down his head he stands, and nose, and ears, and eyesHe smokes, and with his mouth receives the fume that doth arise;Whom followeth straight his wife, and doth the same full solemnly,And of their children every one, and all their family:Which doth preserve, they say, their teeth, and nose, and eyes, and earFrom every kind of malady and sickness all the year.When every one receivéd hath this odor great and small,Then one takes up the pan with coals, and frankincense and all.Another takes the loaf, whom all the rest do follow here,And round about the house they go, with torch or taper clear,That neither bread nor meat do want; nor witch with dreadful charmHave power to hurt their children, or to do their cattle harm.There are that three nights only do perform this foolish gear,To this intent, and think themselves in safety all the year.To Christ dare none commit himself. And in these days besideThey judge what weather all the year shall happen and betide:Ascribing to each day a month, and at this present timeThe youth in every place do flock, and all apparelled fine,With pipers through the streets they run, and sing at every door In commendation of the man, rewarded well therefore,Which on themselves they do bestow, or on the church as thoughThe people were not plagued with rogues and begging friars enow. There cities are where boys and girls together still do run About the streets with like as soon as night begins to come, And bring abroad their wassail-bowls, who well rewarded be With cakes, and cheese, and great good cheer, and money plenteously.

From the German of Thos. Kirchmaier, a.d. 1553.

FOOTNOTE:

[F] White bread.

A PLEA FOR A PRESENT.

Father John Burges,Necessity urgesMy woeful cryTo Sir Robert Pie:And that he will ventureTo send my debenture.Tell him his BenKnew the time whenHe loved the Muses;Though now he refusesTo take apprehensionOf a year's pension,And more is behind;Put him in mindChristmas is near,And neither good cheer,Mirth, fooling, nor wit,Nor any least fitOf gambol or sportWill come to the courtIf there be no money,No plover or conyWill come to the table,Or wine to enableThe muse, or the poet,The parish will know itNor any quick warming-pan help him to bed;If the 'Chequer be empty, so will be his head.

Ben Jonson.

A NEW-YEAR'S GIFT SENT TO SIR SIMEON STEWARD.

No news of navies burnt at sea, No noise of late-spawned Tityries, No closet plot or open vent That frights men with a Parliament: No new device or late-found trick, To read by the stars the kingdom's sick; No gin to catch the State, or wring The free-born nostrils of the king, We send to you, but here a jolly Verse crowned with ivy and with holly; That tells of winter's tales and mirth That milkmaids make about the hearth, Of Christmas sports, the wassail-bowl, That's tost up after fox-i'-th'-hole; Of Blindman-buff, and of the care That young men have to shoe the mare; Of Twelve-tide cake, of peas and beans, Wherewith ye make those merry scenes, When as ye choose your king and queen, And cry out: Hey, for our town green! Of ash-heaps, in the which ye use Husbands and wives by streaks to choose; Of crackling laurel, which foresounds A plenteous harvest to your grounds; Of these and such like things, for shift, We send instead of New-Year's gift: Read then, and when your faces shine With buxom meat and cap'ring wine, Remember us in cups full-crowned, And let our city-health go round, Quite through the young maids and the men To the ninth number, if not ten; Until the fired chestnuts leap For joy to see the fruits ye reap From the plump chalice and the cup That tempts till it be tosséd up. Then, as ye sit about your embers, Call not to mind those fled Decembers; But think on these that are to appear As daughters to the instant year; Sit crowned with rose-buds, and carouse, Till *Liber Pater* twirls the house About your ears; and lay uponThe year, your cares, that's fled and gone.And let the russet swains the ploughAnd harrow hang up resting now;And to the bagpipe all addressTill sleep takes place of weariness;And thus, throughout, with Christmas playsFrolic the full twelve holydays.

Robert Herrick.

THE NEW-YEAR'S GIFT.

Let others look for pearl and goldTissues, or tabbies manifold;One only lock of that sweet hayWhereon the Blessed Baby lay,Or one poor swaddling-clout, shall beThe richest New-Year's gift to me.

Robert Herrick.

AN INVITATION TO THE REVEL.

Come follow, follow me,Those that good fellows be,Into the butteryOur manhood for to try;The master keeps a bounteous house,And gives leave freely to carouse.

Then wherefore should we fear,Seeing here is store of cheer?It shows but cowardiceAt this time to be nice.Then boldly draw your blades and fight,For we shall have a merry night.

When we have done this fray,Then we will go to playAt cards or else at dice,And be rich in a trice;Then let the knaves go round apace,I hope each time to have an ace.

Come, maids, let's want no beerAfter our Christmas cheer,And I will duly craveGood husbands you may have,And that you may good houses keep,When we may drink carouses deep.

And when that's spent the dayWe'll Christmas gambols play,At hot cockles besideAnd then go to all-hide,With many other pretty toys,Men, women, youths, maids, girls, and boys.

Come, let's dance round the hall,And let's for liquor call;Put apples in the fire,Sweet maids, I you desire;And let a bowl be spiced wellOf happy stuff that doth excel.

Twelve days we now have spentIn mirth and merriment,And daintily did fare,For which we took no care:But now I sadly call to mindWhat days of sorrow are behind.

We must leave off to play, To-morrow's working-day; According to each calling Each man must now be falling, And ply his business all the year Next Christmas for to make good cheer.

Now of my master kind Good welcome I did find, And of my loving mistress This merry time of Christmas; For which to them great thanks I give, God grant they long together live.

A CHRISTMAS DITTY.

Sweep the ingle, froth the beer, Tiptoe on till chanticleer, Loose the laugh, dry the tear,—Crack the drums When Christmas comes!

AT THE END OF THE FEAST.

Mark well my heavy, doleful tale, For Twelfth-day now is come, And now I must no longer sing, And say no words but mum; For I perforce must take my leave Of all my dainty cheer, Plum-porridge, roast-beef, and minced-pies, My strong ale and my beer.

Kind-hearted Christmas, now adieu, For I with thee must part, And for to take my leave of thee Doth grieve me at the heart; Thou wert an ancient housekeeper, And mirth with meat didst keep, But thou art going out of town, Which makes me for to weep.

God knoweth whether I again Thy merry face shall see, Which to good fellows and the poor That was so frank and free. Thou lovedst pastime with thy heart, And eke good company; Pray hold me up for fear I swoon, For I am like to die.

Come, butler, fill a brimmer up To cheer my fainting heart, That to old Christmas I may drink Before he doth depart; And let each one that's in this room With me likewise condole, And for to cheer their spirits sad Let each one drink a bowl.

And when the same it hath gone round Then fall unto your cheer, For you do know that Christmas time It comes but once a year. But this good draught which I have drunk Hath comforted my heart, For I was very fearful that My stomach would depart.

Thanks to my master and my dame That doth such cheer afford; God bless them, that each Christmas they May furnish thus their board.My stomach having come to me,I mean to have a bout,Intending to eat most heartily;Good friends, I do not flout.

New Christmas Carols, a.d. 1642.

TWELFTH NIGHT; OR, KING AND QUEEN.

Now, now the mirth comesWith the cake full of plums,Where bean's the king of the sport here;Beside, we must knowThe pea alsoMust revel as queen in the court here.

Begin then to choose,This night, as ye use,Who shall for the present delight here;Be a king by the lot,And who shall notBe Twelve-day queen for the night here!

Which known, let us makeJoy-sops with the cake;And let not a man then be seen here,Who unurged will not drink,To the base from the brink,A health to the king and the queen here!

Next crown the bowl fullWith gentle lamb's wool,And sugar, nutmeg, and ginger,With store of ale, too;And this ye must doTo make the wassail a swinger.

Give then to the kingAnd queen, wassailing,And though with ale ye be wet here,Yet part ye from henceAs free from offenceAs when ye innocent met here

Robert Herrick.

CEREMONIES FOR CANDLEMAS EVE.

Down with the rosemary and bays,Down with the mistletoe;Instead of holly, now upraiseThe greener box for show.

The holly hitherto did sway;Let box now domineerUntil the dancing Easter dayOr Easter's eve appear.

Then youthful box, which now hath graceYour houses to renew,Grown old, surrender must his placeUnto the crispéd yew.

When yew is out, then birch comes in,And many flowers beside,Both of a fresh and fragrant kin,To honor Whitsuntide.

Green rushes then, and sweetest bents,With cooler oaken boughs,Come in for comely ornaments,To readorn the house.Thus times do shift, each thing his turn does hold;New things succeed as former things grow old.

Robert Herrick.

ANOTHER CEREMONY.

Down with the rosemary, and soDown with the bays and mistletoe;Down with the holly, ivy, allWherewith ye dressed the Christmas hall,That so the superstitious findNo one last branch there left behind;For, look! how many leaves there beNeglected there, maids, trust to meSo many goblins you shall see.

Robert Herrick.

THE CEREMONIES FOR CANDLEMAS DAY.

Kindle the Christmas brand, and thenTill sunset let it burn,Which quenched, then lay it up againTill Christmas next return.

Part must be kept, wherewith to teendThe Christmas log next year,And where 'tis safely kept, the fiendCan do no mischief there.

Robert Herrick.

ANOTHER CEREMONY.

End now the white-loaf and the pie, And let all sports with Christmas die.

Robert Herrick.

SAINT DISTAFF'S DAY, THE MORROW AFTER TWELFTH DAY.

Partly work and partly playYe must on St. Distaff's day;From the plough soon free your team,Then come home and fodder them;If the maids a-spinning go,Burn the flax and fire the tow;Scorch their plackets, but bewareThat ye singe no maiden-hair;Bring in pails of water then,Let the maids bewash the men;Give St. Distaff all the right,Then bid Christmas sport good-night,And next morrow every oneTo his own vocation.

Robert Herrick.

The Shepherds.

"His place of birth a solemn angel tellsTo simple shepherds keeping watch by night."

Milton.

ON OATEN PIPES.

As I rode out this enderes night, Of three ioli sheppardes I saw a sight, And all abowte there fold a star shone bright; They sang, terli, terlow; So mereli the sheppardes their pipes can blow.

Doune from heaven, from heaven so hie, Of angeles ther came a great companie, With mirthe, and joy, and great solemnitye, The sange, terly, terlow; So mereli the sheppardes their pipes can blow.

Coventry Mysteries.

PIPE-PLAYING.

Tyrle, Tyrle, so Merrily the Shepherds began to Blow.

About the field they piped full right, Even about the midst of the night; Adown from heaven they saw come a light, *Tyrle, tyrle.*

Of angels there came a company With merry songs and melody, The shepherds anon gan them espy, *Tyrle, tyrle.*

Gloria in excelsis the angels sung, And said how peace was present among, To every man that to the faith would 'long, *Tyrle, tyrle.*

The shepherds hied them to Bethlehem To see that blessed sun's beam; And there they found that glorious stream, *Tyrle, tyrle.*

Now pray we to that meek Child, And to his mother that is so mild, The which was never defiled, *Tyrle, tyrle.*

That we may come unto his bliss, Where joy shall never miss; That we may sing in Paradise, *Tyrle, tyrle.*

I pray you all that be here For to sing and make good cheer, In the worship of God this year, *Tyrle, tyrle.*

Wright's Songs and Carols.

THE FIRST CAROL.

The first Nowell the Angel did sayWas to three poor Shepherds in the fields as they lay;In fields where they lay keeping their sheep,In a cold winter's night that was so deep. *Nowell, Nowell, Nowell, Nowell,Born is the King of Israel.*

They looked up and saw a StarShining in the East beyond them far;And to the earth it gave great light,And so it continued both day and night. *Nowell, Nowell, Nowell, Nowell,Born is the King of Israel.*

And by the light of that same StarThree Wise Men came from country far;To seek for a King was their intent,And to follow the Star wherever it went. *Nowell, Nowell, Nowell, Nowell,Born is the King of Israel.*

The Star drew nigh to the northwest,O'er Bethlehem it took its rest,And there it did both stop and stayRight over the place where Jesus lay. *Nowell, Nowell, Nowell, Nowell,Born is the King of Israel.*

Then did they know assuredlyWithin that house the King did lie:One enter'd in then for to see,And found the Babe in poverty. *Nowell, Nowell, Nowell, Nowell,Born is the King of Israel.*

Then enter'd in those Wise Men threeMost reverently upon their knee,And offer'd there in his presenceBoth gold, and myrrh, and frankincense. *Nowell, Nowell, Nowell, Nowell,Born is the King of Israel.*

Between an ox-stall and an assThis Child truly there born he was;For want of clothing they did him layAll in the manger among the hay. *Nowell, Nowell, Nowell, Nowell, Born is the King of Israel.*

Then let us all with one accordSing praises to our Heavenly Lord,That hath made heaven and earth of naught,And with his blood mankind hath bought. *Nowell, Nowell, Nowell, Nowell, Born is the King of Israel.*

If we in our time shall do well,We shall be free from death and hell;For God hath prepared for us allA resting-place in general. *Nowell, Nowell, Nowell, Nowell, Born is the King of Israel.*

IN BETHLEHEM.

In Bethlehem, that noble place,As by the Prophet said it was,Of the Virgin Mary, filled with grace.*Salvator mundi natus est.*Be we merry in this feast,*In quo Salvator natus est.*

On Christmas night an Angel toldThe shepherds watching by their fold,In Bethlehem, full nigh the wold,"*Salvator mundi natus est.*"Be we merry in this feast,*In quo Salvator natus est.*

The shepherds were encompassed right,About them shone a glorious light,"Dread ye naught," said the Angel bright,"*Salvator mundi natus est.*"Be we merry in this feast,*In quo Salvator natus est.*

"No cause have ye to be afraid,For why? this day is Jesus laidOn Mary's lap, that gentle maid:*Salvator mundi natus est.*Be we merry in this feast,*In quo Salvator natus est.*

"And thus in faith find him ye shallLaid poorly in an ox's stall."The shepherds then lauded God all,*Quia Salvator natus est.*Be we merry in this feast,*In quo Salvator natus est.*

Christmas Carolles, a.d. 1550.

A CAROL IN THE PASTURES.

Sweet music, sweeter farThan any song is sweet:Sweet music, heavenly rare,Mine ears, O peers, doth greet.You gentle flocks, whose fleeces, pearled with dew,Resemble heaven, whom golden drops make bright,Listen, O listen, now, O not to youOur pipes make sport to shorten weary night;But voices most divineMake blissful harmony:Voices that seem to shine,For what else clears the sky?Tunes can we hear, but not the singers see,The tunes divine, and so the singers be.

Lo, how the firmamentWithin an azure foldThe flock of stars hath pent,That we might them behold;Yet from their beams proceedeth not this light,Nor can their crystals such reflection give.What then doth make the element so bright?The heavens are come down upon earth to live.But hearken to the song,Glory to glory's king,And peace all men among,These quiristers do sing.Angels they are, as also (Shepherds) heWhom in our fear we do admire to see.

Let not amazement blindYour souls, said he, annoy:To you and all mankindMy message bringeth joy.For lo, the world's great Shepherd now is bornA blessed babe, an infant full of power:After long night uprisen is the morn,Renowning Bethl'em in the Saviour.Sprung is the perfect day,By prophets seen afar:Sprung is the mirthful May,Which winter cannot mar.In David's city doth this sun appearClouded in flesh, yet, shepherds, sit we here?

Edward Bolton.

A Shepherd

THE SHEPHERDS.

Sweet, harmless livers! on whose holy leisureWaits innocence and pleasure;Whose leaders to those pastures and clear springsWere patriarchs, saints, and kings;How happened it that in the dead of nightYou only saw true light,While Palestine was fast asleep and layWithout one thought of day?Was it because those first and blesséd swainsWere pilgrims on those plainsWhen they received the promise, for which now'Twas there first shown to you?'Tis true he loves that dust whereon they goThat serve him here below,And therefore might for memory of thoseHis love then first disclose;But wretched Salem, once his love, must nowNo voice nor vision know;Her stately piles with all their height and prideNow languishéd and died,And Bethl'em's humble cots above them steptWhile all her seers slept;Her cedar fir, hewed stones, and gold were allPolluted through their fall;And those once sacred mansions were nowMere emptiness and show.This made the angel call at reeds and thatch,Yet where the shepherds watch,And God's own lodging, though he could not lack,To be a common rack.No costly pride, no soft-clothed luxuryIn those thin cells could lie;Each stirring wind and storm blew through their cots,Which never harbored plots;Only content and love and humble joysLived there without all noise;Perhaps some harmless cares for the next dayDid in their bosoms play:As where to lead their sheep, what silent nook,What springs or shades to look;But that was all; and now with gladsome careThey for the town prepare;They leave their flock, and in a busy talkAll towards Bethl'em walk,To seek their soul's great Shepherd who was comeTo bring all stragglers home;Where now they find him out, and, taught before,The Lamb of God adore,That Lamb, whose days great kings and prophets wishedAnd longed to see, but missed.The first light they beheld was bright and gay,And turned their night to day;But to this later light they saw in him,Their day was dark and dim.

Henry Vaughan.

ON SHEPHERDS' PIPES.

O than the fairest day, thrice fairer night!Night to blest days in which a sun doth riseOf which that golden age which clears the skiesIs but a sparkling ray, a shadow-light!And blessed ye, in silly pastors' sight,Mild creatures, in whose warm crib now liesThat heaven-sent youngling, holy-maid-born wight:Midst, end, beginning of our prophecies!Blest cottage that hath flowers in winter spread,Though withered—blessed grass that hath the graceTo deck and be a carpet to that place!Thus sang, unto the sounds, of oaten reed,Before the Babe, the shepherds bowed on knees;And springs ran nectar, honey dropped from trees.

William Drummond.

ANGEL TIDINGS.

Run, shepherds, run where Bethlehem blest appears.We bring the best of news; be not dismayed;A Saviour there is born more old than years,Amidst heaven's rolling height this earth who stayed.In a poor cottage inned, a virgin maidA weakling did him bear, who all upbears;There is he poorly swaddled, in manger laid,To whom too narrow swaddlings are our spheres:Run, shepherds, run, and solemnize his birth.This is that night—no, day, grown great with bliss,In which the power of Satan broken is:In Heaven be glory, peace unto the earth!Thus singing, through the air the angels swam,And cope of stars re-echoéd the same.

William Drummond.

THE NEWS-BEARERS.

The shepherds went their hasty way,And found the lowly stable-shedWhere the Virgin-Mother lay;And now they checked their eager tread,For to the Babe that at her bosom clung,A mother's song the Virgin-Mother sung.

They told her how a glorious light,Streaming from a heavenly throng,Around them shone, suspending night!While sweeter than a mother's song,Blest angels heralded the Saviour's birth,Glory to God on high! and peace on earth!

She listened to the tale divine,And closer still the Babe she prest;And while she cried, the Babe is mine!The milk rushed faster to her breast;Joy rose within her like a summer's morn;Peace, peace on earth! the Prince of peace is born.

Thou Mother of the Prince of peace,Poor, simple, and of low estate!That strife should vanish, battle cease,O why should this thy soul elate?Sweet music's loudest note, the poet's story,—Didst thou ne'er love to hear of fame and glory?

And is not war a youthful king,A stately hero clad in mail?Beneath his footsteps laurels spring;Him earth's majestic monarchs hailTheir friend, their playmate! and his bold bright eyeCompels the maiden's love-confessing sigh.

"Tell this in some more courtly scene,To maids and youths in robes of state!I am a woman poor and mean,And therefore is my soul elate;War is a ruffian all with guilt defiled,That from the aged father tears his child.

"A murderous fiend by fiends adored,He kills the sire and starves the son;The husband kills and from her boardSteals all his widow's toil had won;Plunders God's world of beauty; rends awayAll safety from the night, all comfort from the day.

"Then wisely is my soul elateThat strife should vanish, battle cease;I'm poor and of a low estate,The Mother of the Prince of peace,Joy rises in me, like a summer's morn:Peace, peace on earth! the Prince of peace is born!"

Samuel Taylor Coleridge.

HYMN FOR CHRISTMAS-DAY.

(BEING A DIALOGUE BETWEEN THREE SHEPHERDS.)

Where is this blessed BabeThat hath madeAll the world so full of joyAnd expectation;That glorious boyThat crowns each nationWith a triumphant wreath of blessedness?

Where should he be but in the throng,And amongHis angel ministers, that singAnd take wingJust as may echo to his voice,And rejoice,When wing and tongue and allMay so procure their happiness?

But he hath other waiters now:A poor cow,An ox and mule, stand and behold,And wonderThat a stable should enfoldHim that can thunder.

O what a gracious God have we,How good! how great! even as our misery.

Jeremy Taylor.

A HYMN OF THE NATIVITY.

(SUNG AS BY THE SHEPHERDS.)

Come we shepherds whose blest sightHath met Love's noon in Nature's night;Come, lift we up our loftier song,And wake the sun that lies too long.

To all our world of well-stol'n joy,He slept and dreamt of no such thing,While we found out heaven's fairer eyeAnd kist the cradle of our King;Tell him he rises now too lateTo show us aught worth looking at.

Tell him we now can show him moreThen e'er he showed to mortal sight,Than he himself e'er saw before,Which to be seen needs not his light.Tell him, Tityrus, where th' hast been,Tell him, Thyrsis, what th' hast seen.

Tityrus.

Gloomy night embraced the placeWhere the noble Infant lay,The Babe looked up and showed his face;In spite of darkness it was dayIt was thy day, Sweet, and did riseNot from the East, but from thine eyes.Chorus.—It was thy day, Sweet, etc.

Thyrsis.

Winter chid aloud and sentThe angry North to wage his wars;The North forgot his fierce intent,And left perfumes instead of scars;By those sweet eyes' persuasive powers,Where he meant frost he scattered flowers.Chorus.—By those sweet eyes, etc.

Both.

We saw thee in thy balmy nest,Bright dawn of our eternal day!We saw thine eyes break from their EastAnd chase the trembling shades away;We saw thee, and we blest the sight,We saw thee by thine own sweet light.

Tityrus.

Poor world (said I), what wilt thou doTo entertain this starry stranger?Is this the best thou canst bestow,A cold and not too cleanly manger.Contend, ye powers of heaven and earth,To fit a bed for this huge birth.Chorus.—Contend, ye powers, etc.

Thyrsis.

Proud world (said I), cease your contest,And let the mighty Babe alone;The Phœnix builds the Phœnix nest,Love's architecture is all one.The Babe whose birth embraves this mornMade his own bed ere he was born.Chorus.—The Babe whose birth, etc.

Tityrus.

I saw the curl'd drops, soft and slow,Come hovering o'er the place's head,Offering their whitest sheets of snowTo furnish the fair Infant's bed:Forbear (said I), be not too bold;Your fleece is white, but 'tis too cold.Chorus.—Forbear (said I), etc.

Thyrsis.

I saw the obsequious seraphinsTheir rosy fleece of fire bestow;For well they now can spare their wings,Since heaven itself lies here below:Well done (said I), but are you sureYour down so warm will pass for pure.Chorus.—Well done (said I), etc.

Tityrus.

No, no, your king's not yet to seekWhere to repose his royal head;See, see, how soon his new-bloom'd cheekTwixt's mother's breasts is gone to bed:Sweet choice (said I), no way but so,Not to lie cold, yet sleep in snow.Chorus.—Sweet choice (said I), etc.

Both.

We saw thee in thy balmy nest,Bright dawn of our eternal day!We saw thine eyes break from their EastAnd chase the trembling shades away;We saw thee, and we blest the sight,We saw thee by thine own sweet light.Chorus.—We saw thee, etc.

Full Chorus.

Welcome, all wonder in one sight,Eternity shut in a span,Summer in winter, day in night,Heaven in earth and God in man!Great little One! whose all-embracing birthLifts earth to heaven, stoops heaven to earth.

Welcome, though not to gold nor silk,To more than Cæsar's birthright is,Two Sister Seas of Virgin milkWith many a rarely-tempered kiss,That breathes at once both Maid and Mother,Warms in the one and cools in the other.

She sings thy tears asleep, and dipsHer kisses in thy weeping eye;She spreads the red leaves of thy lipsThat in their buds yet blushing lie:She 'gainst those mother-diamonds triesThe points of her young eagle's eyes.

Welcome, though not to those gay fliesGilded i' the beams of earthly kings,Slippery souls in smiling eyes,But to poor shepherds' homespun things;Whose wealth's their flock, whose wit to beWell read in their simplicity.

Yet when young April's husband-showersShall bless the fruitful Maia's bed,We'll bring the first-born of her flowersTo kiss thy feet and crown thy head:To thee, dread Lamb, whose love must keepThe shepherds more than they their sheep.

To thee, meek Majesty! soft KingOf simple graces and sweet loves,Each of us his lamb will bring,Each his pair of silver doves,Till burnt at last in fire of thy fair eyesOurselves become our own best sacrifice.

Richard Crashaw.

SUNG BY THE SHEPHERD.

The New Year is begun,Good-morrow, my masters all!The cheerful rising sunNow shining in this hall,Brings mirth and joyTo man and boy.With all that here doth dwell;Whom Jesus blessWith love's increase,So all things shall prosper well.

A New-Year's gift I bringUnto my master here,Which is a welcome thingOf mirth and merry cheer.A New-Year's lambCome from thy damAn hour before daybreak,Your noted eweDoth this bestow,Good master, for your sake.

And to my dame so kindThis New-Year's gift I bring;I'll bear an honest mindUnto her whilst I live.Your white-woolled sheepI'll safely keepFrom harm of bush or brere,That garments gayFor your arrayMay clothe you the next New Year.

And to your children all,These New-Year's gifts I bring;And though the price be small,They're fit for queen or king:Fair pippins redKept in my bedA-mellowing since last year,Whose beauty brightSo clear of sightTheir hearts will glad and cheer.

And to your maids and menI bring both points and pins;Come bid me welcome then,The good New Year begins:And for my loveLet me approveThe friendship of your Maid,Whose nappy ale,So good and stale,Will make my wits afraid.

I dare not with it dealBut in a sober diet:If I, poor shepherd, stealA draught to be unquiet,And lose my wayThis New-Year's dayAs I go to my fold,You'll surely thinkMy love of drinkThis following year will hold.

Here stands my bottle and hook,Good kitchen-maid, draw near,Thou art an honest cook,And canst brew ale and beer;Thy office show,Before I go,My bottle and bag come fill,And for thy sakeI'll merry makeUpon the next green hill.

New Christmas Carols.

FROM "THE LIGHT OF THE WORLD."

AT BETHLEHEM.

So many hills arising, green and gray,On Earth's large round, and that one hill to say:"I was his bearing-place!" On Earth's wide breastSo many maids! and she—of all most blest—Heavily mounting Bethlehem, to beHis Mother!—Holy Maid of Galilee!Hill, with the olives, and the little town!If rivers from their crystal founts flow down,If 'twas the dawn which did day's gold unbar,Ye were beginnings of the best we are,The most we see, the highest that we know,The lifting heavenward of man's life below.Therefore, though better lips ye shall not lack,Suffer if one of modern mood steals back—Weary and wayworn from the desert-roadOf barren thought; from Hope's Dead Sea, which glowedWith Love's fair mirage; from the poet's haunt,The scholar's lamp, the statesman's scheme, the vaunt,The failure, of all fond philosophies,—Back unto Thee, back to thy olive-trees,Thy people, and thy story, and thy Son,Mary of Nazareth! So long agoneBearing us Him who made our christendom,And came to save the earth, from heav'n, His home.

So many hill-sides, crowned with rugged rocks!So many simple shepherds keeping flocksIn many moonlit fields! but, only they—So lone, so long ago, so far away—On that one winter's night, at Bethlehem,To have white angels singing lauds for them!They only—hinds wrapped in the he-goat's skin—To hear heaven's music, bidding peace begin!Only for those, of countless watching eyes,The "Glory of the Lord" glad to arise;The skies to blaze with gold and silver lightOf seraphs by strong joy flashed into sight;The wind, for them, with that strange song to swell,—By too much happiness incredible—That tender anthem of good times to be,Then at their dawn—not daylight yet, ah me!"Peace upon earth! Good-will!" sung to the stringsOf lutes celestial. Nay, if these thingsToo blessëd to believe have seemed, or seem,Not ours the fault, dear angels! Prove the dreamWaking and true! Sing once again, and makeMoonlight and starlight sweet for earth's sad sake!Or, if heaven bids ye lock in silence stillConquest of peace, and coming of good-will,Till times to be, then—oh, you placid sheep!Ah, thrice-blest shepherds! suffer if we creepBack through the tangled thicket of the yearsTo graze in your fair flock, to strain our earsWith listening herdsmen, if, perchance, one noteOf such high singing in the fine air float;If any rock thrills yet with that great strainWe did not hear, and shall not hear, again;If any olive-leaf at BethlehemLisps still one syllable vouchsafed to them;If some stream, conscious still—some breeze—be stirredWith echo of th' immortal words ye heard.

What was it that ye heard? the wind of nightPlaying in cheating tones, with touches light,Amid the palm-plumes? or, one stop outblownOf planetary music, so far flownEarthwards, that to those innocent ears 'twas brought Which bent the mighty measure to their thought?Or, haply, from breast-shaped Beth-Haccarem,The hill of Herod, some waft sent to themOf storming drums and trumps, at festivalHeld in the Idumæan's purple hall?Or, it may be, some Aramaic songOf country lovers, after partings longMeeting anew, with much "good will" indeed,Blown by some swain upon his Jordan reed?Nay, nay! your abbas back ye did not fling,From each astonished ear, for swains to singTheir village-verses clear; for sounds well-knownOf wandering breeze, or whispering trees, or toneOf Herod's trumpets. And ye did not gazeHeart-startled on the stars (albeit the raysOf that lone orb shot, sparkling, from the eastUnseen before), for these, largest and least,Were fold-lamps, lighted nightly: and ye knewFar differing glory in the night's dark blueSuddenly lit with rose, and pierced with spikeOf golden spear-beam. Oh, a dream, belike!Some far-fetched vision, new to peasant's sleep,Of paradise stripped bare!—But, why thus keepSecrets for them? This bar, which doth encloseBetter and nobler souls, why burst for those Who supped on the parched pulse, and lapped the stream,And each, at the same hour, dreams the same dream!Or, easier still, they lied! Yet, wherefore, then"Rise, and go up to Bethlehem," and unpenTo wolf and jackal all their hapless foldSo they might "see these things which had been toldIn heaven's own voice"? And heaven, whate'er betide,Spreads surely somewhere, on death's farther side!

And, truly, if joy's music once hath rungFrom lips of bands invisible, if any— (Be they the dead, or of the deathless many)— Love and serve man, angelical befrienders,Glad of his weal, and from his woe defenders,—If such, in heaven, have pity on our tears,Forever falling with the unmending years,High cause had they, at Bethlehem, that night,To lift the curtain of hope's hidden light,To break decree of silence with love's cry,Foreseeing how this Babe, born lowlily,Should—past dispute, since now achieved is this—Bring earth great gifts of blessing and of bliss;Date, from that crib, the dynasty of love;Strip his misusëd thunderbolts from Jove;Bend to their knee Rome's Cæsars, break the chainFrom the slave's neck; set sick hearts free againBitterly bound by priests, and scribes, and scrolls;And heal, with balm of pardon, sinking souls:Should mercy to her vacant throne restore,Teach right to kings, and patience to the poor;Should, from that bearing-cave, outside the khan,Amid the kneeling cattle, rise, and beLight of all lands, and splendor of each sea,The sun-burst of a new morn come to earth,Not yet, alas! broad day, but day's white birthWhich promiseth; and blesseth, promising.These from that night! What cause of wonderingIf that one silence of all silencesBrake into music? if, for hopes like theseAngels, who love us, sang that song, and showOf time's far purpose made the "great light" glow?

Wherefore, let whosoever will drink dryHis cup of faith; and think that, verily,Not in a vision, no way otherwiseThan those poor shepherds told, there did ariseThis portent. Being amidst their sheep and goats,Lapped careless in their pasture-keeping coats,Blind as their drowsy beasts to what drew nigh, (Such the lulled ear, and such th' unbusied eyeWhich ofttimes hears and sees hid things!) there spreadThe "Glory of the Lord" around each head:Broke, be it deemed, o'er hill and over hollow,On the inner seeing, the sense concealed, unknown,Of those plain hinds—glad, humble, and alone—Flooding their minds, filling their hearts; around,Above, below, disclosing grove and ground,The rocks, the hill, the town, the solitude,The wondering flocks,—agaze with grass half-chewed,—The palm-crowns, and the path to Bethlehem,As sight angelic spies. And, came to themThe "Angel of the Lord," visible, sure,Known for the angel by his presence pureWhereon was written love, and peace, and grace,With beauty passing mortal mien and face.

So when the Angels were no more to see, Re-entering those gates of space,—whose key Love keeps on that side, and on this side death— Each shepherd to the other whispering saith, Lest he should miss some lingering symphonies Of that departing music, "Let us rise And go even now to Bethlehem, and spy This which is come to pass, shewed graciously By the Lord's angels." Therewith hasted they By olive-yards, and old walls mossed and gray Where, in close chinks, the lizard and the snake, Thinking the sunlight come, stirred, half-awake: Across the terraced levels of the vines, Under the pillared palms, along the lines Of lance-leaved oleanders, scented sweet, Through the pomegranate-gardens sped their feet; Over the causeway, up the slope, they spring, Breast the steep path, with steps not slackening; Past David's well, past the town-wall they ran, Unto the House of Chimham, to the khan, Where mark them peering in, the posts between, Questioning—all out of breath—if birth hath been This night, in any guest-room, high or low? The drowsy porter at the gate saith, "No!"—Shooting the bars; while the packed camels shake Their bells to listen, and the sleepers wake, And to their feet the ponderous steers slow rise, Lifting from trampled fodder large mild eyes;—"Nay! Brothers! no such thing! yet there is gone Yonder, one nigh her time, a gentle one! With him that seemed her spouse—of Galilee; They toiled at sundown to our doors—but, see! No nook was here! Seek at the cave instead; We shook some barley-straw to make their bed."

Then to the cave they wended, and there spied That which was more, if truth be testified, Than all the pomp seen thro' proud Herod's porch Ablaze with brass, and silk, and scented torch, High on Beth-Haccarem; more to behold, If men had known, than all the glory toldOf splendid Cæsar in his marbled homeOn the white Isle; or audience-hall at RomeWith trembling princes thronged. A clay lamp swingsBy twisted camel-cords, from blackened rings,Shewing with flickering gleams, a Child new-bornWrapped in a cloth, laid where the beasts at mornWill champ their bean-straw: in the lamp-ray dimA fresh-made Mother by Him, fostering HimWith face and mien to worship, speaking naught;Close at hand Joseph, and the ass, hath broughtThat precious twofold burden to the gate;With goats, sheep, oxen, driven to shelter late:No mightier sight! Yet all sufficeth it—If we will deem things be beyond our wit—To prove heaven's music true, and show heaven's way,How, not by famous kings, nor with arrayOf brazen letters on the boastful stone,But "by the mouth of babes," quiet, alone,Little beginnings planning for large ends,With other purpose than fond man attends,Wisdom and love, in secret fellowshipGuide our world's wandering with a finger-tip;And how, that night, as these did darkly see,They sealed the first scrolls of earth's history,And opened what shall run till death be dead.

Which babe they reverenced, bending low the head,First of all worshippers; and told the thingsDone in the plain, and played on angel's strings.Then those around wondered and worshipped, too,And Mary heard—but wondered not—anewHiding this in her heart, the heart which beatWith blood of Jesus Christ, holy and sweet.

Also, not marvelling, albeit they heard,Stood certain by—those three swart ones—appearedFrom climes unknown; yet, surely, on high questOf what that star proclaimed, bright on the breastFirst of the Ram, afterwards glittering thenceInto the watery Trigon, where, intense,It lit the Crab, and burned the Fishes pale.Three Signiors, owning many a costly bale;Three travelled masters, by their bearing lordsOf lands and slaves. The Indian silk affords,With many a folded braid of white and gold,Shade to their brows; rich goat-hair shawls did foldTheir gowns of flow'r'd white muslin, midway tied;And ruby, turkis, emerald—stones of pride—Blazed on their thumb-rings; and a pearl gleamed whiteIn every ear; and silver belts, clasped tight,Held ink-box, reeds, and knives, in scabbards gemmed;Curled shoes of goat-skin dyed, with seed-pearls hemmed,Shod their brown feet; hair shorn; lids low, to think—Eyes deep and wistful, as of those who drinkWaters of hidden wisdom, night and day,And live twain lives, conforming as they may,In diligence, and due observancesTo ways of men; yet, not at one with these;But ever straining past the things that seemTo that which is—the truth behind the dream.Three princely wanderers of the Asian bloodPerchance, by Indus dwellers; or some flood,That feeds her from Himâla's icy dome;Or, haply, to those Syrian palm-trees comeFrom Gunga's banks, or mounts of MalabarWhich lift the Deccan to its sun, and far—Rampart-like—fringe the blue Arabian Sea.True followers of the Buddh they seemed to be,The better arm and shoulder showing bareWith each; and on the neck of each, draped fairA scarf of saffron, patched; and, 'twixt the eyes,In saffron stamped, the Name of mysteriesOM; and the Swastika, with secrets rifeHow man may 'scape the dire deceits of life.

These three stood by, as who would entrance make;And heard the shepherd's tale; and, hearing, spakeStrange Indian words one to another; then sentCommand. Their serving-men, obedient,Cast loose from off the camels, kneeling nigh,Nettings and mats, and made the fastenings flyFrom belly-band, and crupper-rope, and tail;And broke the knots, and let each dusty baleSlide from the saddle-horns, and give to seeLong-hoarded treasure of great jewelry,And fragrant secrets of the Indian grove,And splendors of the Indian looms, inwoveWith gold and silver flowers: "for, now," said they,"Our eyes have seen.this thing sought day by day;By the all-conscious, silent sky well-known,And, specially, of yon white star fore-shownWhich, bursting magically on the sight,Beckoned us from our homes, shining aright,The silver beacon to this holy hill:Mark if it sparkles not, aware and still,Over the place: The astral houses, see!Spake truth: Our feet were guided faithfully.'Tis the Star-Child, who was to rise, and wearA crown than Suleiman's more royal and rare,'King of the Jews!' Grant an approach to usWho crave to worship Him."

Now, it fell thusThat these first to Jerusalem had passed,And sojourned there, observing feast and fastIn the thronged city; oft of townsmen seenIn market and bazaar; and, by their mienNoted for lordliest of all strangers there,Much whispered of, in sooth, as who saw clearShadows of times to come, and secrets brightWrit in the jewelled cipher of the night.So that the voice of this to Herod wentFeastful and fearful; ever ill-contentMid plots and perils; girt with singing boys,And dancing girls of Tyre, and armored noiseOf Cæsar's legionaries. Long and near,In audience hall, each dusky wayfarerQuestioned he of their knowledge, and the star, What message flashed it? Whether near or far Would rise this portent of a Babe to reign King of the Jews, and bring a crown again To weeping Zion, and cast forth from them The Roman scourge? And if at Bethlehem, As, with one voice, priests, elders, scribes aver, Then, let them thither wend, and spy the stir, And find this Babe, and come anew to him, Declaring where the wonder. "'Twas his whim" Quotha "to be of fashion with the stars, (Weary, like them, of gazing upon wars) To shine upon this suckling, bending knee Save unto Cæsar uncrooked latterly."

Thence came it those three stood at entering Before the door; and their rich gifts did bring, Red gold from the Indian rocks, cunningly beat To plate and chalice, with old fables sweet Of Buddh's compassion, and dark Mara's powers Round the brims glittering; and a riot of flowers Done on the gold, with gold script to proclaim The Noble Truths, and Threefold mystic Name OM, and the Swastika, and how man wins Blessed Nirvana's rest, being quit of sins, And, day and night, reciting, "Oh, the Gem! Upon the Lotus! Oh, the Lotus-stem!" Also, more precious than much gold, they poured Rare spices forth, unknitting cord on cord; And, one by one, unwinding cloths, as though The merchantmen had sought to shut in so The breath of those distillings: in such kind As when Nile's black embalming slaves would bind Sindon o'er sindon, cere-cloth, cinglets, bands Roll after roll, on head, breast, feet, and hands, Round some dead king, whose cold and withered palm Had dropped the sceptre; drenched with musk and balm, And natron, and what keeps from perishing; So they might save—after long wandering—The body for the spirit, and hold fast Life's likeness, till the dead man lived at last.Thus, from their coats involved of leaves and silk,Slowly they freed the odorous thorn-tree's milk,The gray myrrh, and the cassia, and the spice,Filling the wind with frankincense past price,With hearts of blossoms from a hundred glensAnd essence of a thousand rose-gardens,Till the night's gloom like a royal curtain hungJewelled with stars, and rich with fragrance flungAthwart the arch; and, in the cavern thereThe air around was as the breathing-airOf a queen's chamber, when she comes to bed,And all that glad earth owns gives goodlihead.

Witness them entering,—these three from afar—Who knew the skies, and had the strange white starTo light their nightly lamp, thro' deserts wideOf Bactria, and the Persic wastes, and tideOf Tigris and Euphrates; past the snowOf Ararat, and where the sand-winds blowO'er Ituræa; and the crimson peaksOf Moab, and the fierce, bright, barren reeksFrom Asphaltites; to this hill—to theeBethlehem-Ephrata! Witness these threeGaze, hand in hand, with faces grave and mild,Where, 'mid the gear and goats, Mother and ChildMake state and splendor for their eyes. Then layEach stranger on the earth, in the Indian way,Paying the "eight prostrations;" and was heardSaying softly, in the Indian tongue, that wordWherewith a Prince is honored. Humbly ran,On this, the people of their caravanAnd fetch the gold, and—laid on gold—the spice,Frankincense, myrrh: and next, with reverence nice,Foreheads in dust, they spread the precious thingsAt Mary's feet, and worship Him who clingsTo Mary's bosom drinking soft life soWho shall be life and light to all below."For, now we see," say they, departing: "plainThe star's word comes to pass! The Buddh againAppeareth, or some Bôddhisat of mightArising for the west, who shall set right,And serve and reconcile; and, maybe, teachKnowledge to those who know. We, brothers, each,Have heard yon shepherds babbling: if the skySpeaketh with such, heaven's mercy is drawn nigh!Well did we counsel, journeying to this place!Yon hour-old Babe, milking that breast of grace,The world will praise and worship, well-content."

Then, fearing Herod, to their homes they wentMusing along the road. But he alwayAngered and troubled, bade his soldiers slayWhatever man-child sucked in Bethlehem.Lord! had'st Thou been all God, as pleaseth themWho poorly see Thy godlike self, and takeTrue glory from Thee for false glory's sake:Co-equal power, as these—too bold—blaspheme,Ruler of what Thou camest to redeem;Not Babe Divine, feeling with touch of silkFor fountains of a mortal Mother's milkWith sweet mouth buried in the warm feast thus,And dear heart growing great to beat for us,And soft feet waiting till the way was spreadWhereby what was true God in Thee should treadTriumphant over woe and death to bliss,—Thou, from Thy cradle would'st have stayed in thisThose butchers! With one angel's swift decree,Out of the silver cohorts lackeying Thee,Thou had'st thrust down the bitter prince who killedThine innocents! Would'st Thou not? Was't not willed?Alas! "Peace and good-will" in agonyFound first fruits! Rama heard that woful cryOf Rachel weeping for the children; lone,Uncomforted, because her babes are gone.Herod the King! hast thou heard Rachel's wailWhere restitution is? Did aught availSomewhere? at last? past life? after long stressOf heavy shame to bring forgetfulness?If such grace be, no hopeless sin is wrought;Thy bloody blade missed what its vile edge sought;Mother, and Child, and Joseph—safe from thee—Journey to Egypt, while the eastern ThreeWind homewards, lightened of their spice and gold;And those great days, that were to be, unfoldIn the fair fields beside the shining seaWhich rolls, 'mid palms and rocks, in Galilee.

Sir Edwin Arnold.

It Brings Good Cheer.

"You may talk of Country Christmasses,
Their thirty pound butter'd eggs, their pies of carps' tongues;
Their pheasants drench'd with ambergris; the carcasses of three
fat wethers bruised for gravy to make sauce for a single peacock!"

Massinger.

OLD CHRISTMAS RETURNED.

All you that to feasting and mirth are inclined,Come, here is good news for to pleasure your mind;Old Christmas is come for to keep open house,He scorns to be guilty of starving a mouse.Then come, boys, and welcome for diet the chief,Plum-pudding, goose, capon, minced-pies, and roast-beef.

A long time together he hath been forgot,They scarce could afford to hang on the pot;Such miserly sneaking in England hath been,As by our forefathers ne'er us'd to be seen;But now he's returned, you shall have in brief,Plum-pudding, goose, capon, minced-pies, and roast-beef.

The times were ne'er good since Old Christmas was fled,And all hospitality hath been so dead;No mirth at our festivals late did appear,They scarcely would part with a cup of March beer;[Pg 180]But now you shall have for the ease of your grief,Plum-pudding, goose, capon, minced-pies, and roast-beef.

The butler and baker, they now may be glad,The times they are mended, though they have been bad;The brewer, he likewise may be of good cheer,He shall have good trading for ale and strong beer;All trades shall be jolly, and have for relief,Plum-pudding, goose, capon, minced-pies, and roast-beef.

The holly and ivy about the walls wind,And show that we ought to our neighbors be kind,Inviting each other for pastime and sport,And where we best fare, there we most do resort;We fail not of victuals, and that of the chief,Plum-pudding, goose, capon, minced-pies, and roast-beef.

The cooks shall be busied by day and by night, In roasting and boiling, for taste and delight; Their senses in liquor that's nappy they'll steep, Though they be afforded to have little sleep; They still are employed for to dress us in brief, Plum-pudding, goose, capon, minced-pies, and roast-beef.

Although the cold weather doth hunger provoke, 'Tis a comfort to see how the chimneys do smoke; Provision is making for beer, ale, and wine, For all that are willing or ready to dine: Then haste to the kitchen for diet the chief, Plum-pudding, goose, capon, minced-pies, and roast-beef.

All travellers, as they do pass on their way, At gentlemen's halls are invited to stay, Themselves to refresh, and their horses to rest, Since that he must be Old Christmas's guest; Nay, the poor shall not want, but have for relief, Plum-pudding, goose, capon, minced-pies, and roast-beef.

Now Mock-beggar-hall it no more shall stand empty, But all shall be furnisht with freedom and plenty; The hoarding old misers, who us'd to preserve The gold in their coffers, and see the poor starve, Must now spread their tables, and give them in brief, Plum-pudding, goose, capon, minced-pies, and roast-beef.

The court, and the city, and country are glad, Old Christmas is come to cheer up the sad; Broad pieces and guineas about now shall fly, And hundreds be losers by cogging a die, Whilst others are feasting with diet the chief, Plum-pudding, goose, capon, minced-pies, and roast-beef.

Those that have no coin at the cards for to play, May sit by the fire and pass time away, And drink of their moisture contented and free, "My honest, good fellow, come, here is to thee!" And when they are hungry, fall to their relief, Plum-pudding, goose, capon, minced-pies, and roast-beef.

Young gallants and ladies shall foot it along, Each room in the house to the music shall throng, Whilst jolly carouses about they shall pass, And each country swain trip about with his lass; Meantime goes the caterer to fetch in the chief, Plum-pudding, goose, capon, minced-pies, and roast-beef.

The cooks and the scullion, who toil in their frocks, Their hopes do depend upon their Christmas-box; There is very few that do live on the earth But enjoy at this time either profit or mirth; Yea, those that are charged to find all relief, Plum-pudding, goose, capon, minced-pies, and roast-beef.

Then well may we welcome Old Christmas to town, Who brings us good cheer and good liquor so brown; To pass the cold winter away with delight, We feast it all day, and we frolic all night; Both hunger and cold we keep out with relief, Plum-pudding, goose, capon, minced-pies, and roast-beef.

Then let all curmudgeons who dote on their wealth, And value their treasure much more than their health, Go hang themselves up, if they will be so kind; Old Christmas with them but small welcome shall find; They will not afford to themselves without grief, Plum-pudding, goose, capon, minced-pies, and roast-beef.

Evans' Old Ballads.

THE TRENCHERMAN.

My master and dame, I well perceive, Are purposed to be merry to-night, And willingly hath given me leaveTo combat with a Christmas Knight. Sir Pig, I see, comes prancing inAnd bids me draw if that I dare; I care not for his valor a pin, For Jack of him will have a share.

My lady goose among the restupon the table takes her place, And piping-hot bids do my best, And bravely looks me in the face; For pigs and geese are gallant cheer, God bless my master and dame therefore! I trust before the next New YearTo eat my part of half a score.

I likewise see good minced-pieHere standing swaggering on the table; The lofty walls so large and highI'll level down if I be able; For they be furnished with good plums, And spiced well with pepper and salt, Every prune as big as both my thumbsTo drive down bravely the juice of malt.

Fill me some of your Christmas beer, Your pepper sets my mouth on heat, And Jack's a-dry with your good cheer, Give me some good ale to my meat. And then again my stomach I'll show, For good roast-beef here stoutly stands; I'll make it stoop before I go, Or I'll be no man of my hands.

And for the plenty of this houseGod keep it thus well-stored alway; Come, butler, fill me a good carouse, And so we'll end our Christmas day.

New Christmas Carols.

BAN AND BLESSING.

Now Christmas comes, 'tis fit that weShould feast and sing and merry be,Keep open house, let fiddlers play;A fig for cold, sing care away!And may they who thereat repine,On brown bread and on small beer dine.Make fires with logs, let the cooks sweatWith boiling and with roasting meat;Let ovens be heat for fresh suppliesOf puddings, pasties, and minced-pies.And whilst that Christmas doth abideLet butt'ry-door stand open wide.Hang up those churls that will not feastOr with good fellows be a guest,And hang up those would take awayThe observation of that day;O may they never minced-pies eat,Plum-pudding, roast-beef, nor such meat.But blest be they, awake and sleep,Who at that time a good house keep;May never want come nigh their door,Who at that time relieve the poor;Be plenty always in their houseOf beef, veal, lamb, pork, mutton, souse.

Poor Robin's Almanac.

THRICE WELCOME!

Now thrice welcome, Christmas, Which brings us good cheer, Minced-pies and plum porridge, Good ale and strong beer; With pig, goose, and capon, The best that may be, So well doth the weather And our stomachs agree.

Observe how the chimneys Do smoke all about; The cooks are providing For dinner, no doubt; But those on whose tables No victuals appear, O may they keep Lent All the rest of the year.

With holly and ivy So green and so gay, We deck up our houses As fresh as the day; With bay and rosemary And laurel complete; And every one now Is a king in conceit.

Poor Robin's Almanac.

CHRISTMAS PROVENDER.

Provide for Christmas ere that it do come, To feast thy neighbor good cheer to have some; Good bread and drink, a fire in the hall, Brawn, pudding, souse, and good mustard withal. Beef, mutton, pork, and shred pies of the best, Pig, veal, goose, capon, and turkey well drest; Apples and nuts to throw about the hall, That boys and girls may scramble for them all. Sing jolly carols, make the fiddlers play, Let scrupulous fanatics keep away; For oftentimes seen no arranter knave Than some who do counterfeit most to be grave.

Poor Robin's Almanac.

GLEE AND SOLACE.

With merry glee and solaceThis second day of ChristmasNow comes in bravely to my master's house,Where plenty of good cheer I see,With that which most contenteth me,As brawn and bacon, powdered beef, and souse.

For the love of Stephen,That blessed saint of heaven,Which stonéd was for Jesus Christ his sake,Let us all, both more and less,Cast away all heaviness,And in a sober manner merry make.

He was a man belovéd,And his faith approvédBy suffering death on this holy day,Where he with gentle patienceAnd a constant sufferance,Hath taught us all to heaven the ready way.

So let our mirth be civil,That not one thought of evilMay take possession of our hearts at all,So shall we love and favor getOf them that kindly thus do setTheir bounties here so freely in this hall.

Of delicates so dainty,I see now here is plentyUpon this table ready here prepared;Then let us now give thanks to thoseThat all things friendly thus bestows,Esteeming not this world that is so hard.

For of the same my masterHath made me here a taster;The Lord above requite him for the same!And so to all within this houseI will drink a full carouse,With leave of my good master and my dame.

And the Lord be praisedMy stomach is well eased,My bones at quiet may go take their rest;Good fortune surely follow meTo bring me thus so luckilyTo eat and drink so freely of the best.

New Christmas Carols, a.d. 1661.

ON SAINT JOHN'S DAY.

In honor of Saint John we thusDo keep good Christmas cheer;And he that comes to dine with us,I think he need not spare.The butcher he hath killed good beef,The caterer brings it in;But Christmas pies are still the chief,If that I durst begin.

Our bacon-hogs are full and fatTo make us brawn and souse;Full well may I rejoice thereatTo see them in the house.But yet the minced-pie it isThat sets my teeth on water;Good mistress, let me have a bit,For I do long thereafter.

And I will fetch you water inTo brew and bake withal,Your love and favor still to winWhen as you please to call.Then grant me, dame, your love and leaveTo taste your pie-meat here;It is the best, in my conceit,Of all your Christmas-cheer.

he cloves, and mace, and gallant plumsThat here on heaps do lie,And prunes as big as both my thumbs,Enticeth much mine eye.Oh, let me eat my belly-fullOf your good Christmas-pie;Except thereat I have a pull,I think I sure shall die.

Good master, stand my loving friend,For Christmas-time is short,And when it comes unto an endI may no longer sport;Then while it doth continue here,Let me such labor findTo eat my fill of that good cheerThat best doth please my mind.

Then I shall thank my dame therefore,That gives her kind consentThat Jack, your boy, with others more,May have this Christmas spentIn pleasant mirth and merry glee,As young men most delight;For that's the only sport for me,And so God give you all good-night.

New Christmas Carols, a.d. 1661.

CHRISTMAS ALMS.

Now that the time is come whereinOur Saviour Christ was born,The larders full of beef and pork,The garners filled with corn;As God hath plenty to thee sent,Take comfort of thy labors,And let it never thee repentTo feast thy needy neighbors.

Let fires in every chimney beThat people they may warm them;Tables with dishes covered,—Good victuals will not harm them.With mutton, veal, beef, pig, and pork,Well furnish every board;Plum-pudding, furmety, and whatThy stock will them afford.

No niggard of thy liquor be,Let it go round thy table;People may freely drink, but notSo long as they are able.Good customs they may be abused,Which makes rich men to slack us;This feast is to relieve the poor,And not to drunken Bacchus.

This, if thou doest,'Twill credit raise thee;God will thee bless,And neighbors praise thee.

Poor Robin's Almanac.

CHRISTMAS AT THE ROUND TABLE.

The great King Arthur made a royal feast,And held his Royal Christmas at Carlisle,And thither came the vassals, most and least,From every corner of the British Isle;And all were entertained, both man and beast,According to their rank, in proper style;The steeds were fed and littered in the stable,The ladies and the knights sat down to table.

The bill of fare (as you may well suppose)Was suited to those plentiful old times,Before our modern luxuries arose,With truffles, and ragouts, and various crimes;And, therefore, from the original in prose I shall arrange the catalogue in rhymes:They served up salmon, venison and wild boarsBy hundreds, and by dozens, and by scores.

Hogsheads of honey, kilderkins of mustard,Muttons, and fatted beeves, and bacon swine;Herons and bitterns, peacocks, swan, and bustard,Teal, mallard, pigeons, widgeons, and, in fine.Plum-puddings, pancakes, apple-pies, and custard,And therewithal they drank good Gascon wine,With mead, and ale, and cider of our own;For porter, punch, and negus were not known.

All sorts of people there were seen together,All sorts of characters, all sorts of dresses;The fool with fox's tail and peacock feather,Pilgrims, and penitents, and grave burgesses;The country people with their coats of leather,Vintners and victuallers with cans and messes,Grooms, archers, varlets, falconers, and yeomen,Damsels, and waiting-maids, and waiting-women.

John Hookham Frere.

Lullaby.

"Sleep, my little one, Sleep, my pretty one, Sleep."

Tennyson.

A CAROL AT THE MANGER.

Lully, lulla, thow littel tine child;By, by, lully, lullay, thow littell tyne child;By, by, lully, lullay.

O sisters too! how may we do,For to preserve this dayThis pore yongling, for whom we do singBy, by, lully, lullay.

Herod the King, in his raging,Chargid he hath this dayHis men of might, in his owne sight,All yonge children to slay.

That wo is me, pore child for the!And ever morne and day,For the parting nether say nor singeBy, by, lully, lullay.

Coventry Mysteries.

A Vision

A DREAM CAROL.

Ah, my dear Son, said Mary, ah, my dear,Kiss thy mother, Jesu, with a laughing cheer!

This endnes[G] night I saw a sightAll in my sleep,Mary, that May, she sung lullayAnd sore did weep;To keep, she sought, full fast aboutHer Son from cold.Joseph said, Wife, my joy, my life,Say what ye would.Nothing, my spouse, is in this houseUnto my pay;[H]My Son a king, that made all thing,Lieth in hay.Ah, my dear Son! etc.

My mother dear, amend your cheerAnd now be still;Thus for to lie it is soothlyMy Father's will.Derision, great passion,Infinitely,As it is found many a woundSuffer shall I;On Calvary that is so highThere shall I be,Man to restore, nailéd full soreUpon a tree.Ah, my dear Son! etc.

Sandy's Christmas Carols.

FOOTNOTES:

[G]Last.

[H]Content.

THE KING IN THE CRADLE.

My sweet little baby, what meanest thou to cry?Be still, my blesséd babe, though cause thou hast to mourn,Whose blood most innocent to shed the cruel king hath sworn;And lo, alas! behold what slaughter he doth make,Shedding the blood of infants all, sweet Saviour, for thy sake.A King, a King is born, they say, which King this king would kill:O woe and woful heavy day when wretches have their will!Lulla, la lulla, lulla lullaby.

Three kings this King of kings to see are come from far,To each unknown, with offerings great, by guiding of a star;And shepherds heard the song, which angels bright did sing,Giving all glory unto God for coming of this King,Which must be made away—King Herod would him kill;O woe and woful heavy day when wretches have their will?Lulla, etc.

Lo, lo, my little babe, be still, lament no more;From fury thou shalt step aside, help have we still in store:We heavenly warning have some other soil to seek;From death must fly the Lord of life, as lamb both mild and meek:Thus must my babe obey the king that would him kill;O woe and woful heavy day when wretches have their will!Lulla, etc.

But thou shalt live and reign, as sibyls hath foresaid,As all the prophets prophesy, whose mother, yet a maidAnd perfect virgin pure, with her breasts shall upbreedBoth God and man that all hath made, the son of heavenly seed:Whom caitives none can

'tray, whom tyrants none can kill:O joy and joyful happy day
when wretches want their will!Lulla, etc.

Byrd's Psalmes, Sonets, etc., a.d. 1588.

MADONNA AND CHILD.

This endris night[I]I saw a sight,A star as bright as day;And ever amongA maiden sung,Lullay, by by, lullay.

This lovely lady sat and sang, and to her child she said,—"My son, my brother, my father dear, why liest thou thus in hayd?[J]My sweet bird,Thus it is betideThough thou be king veray;But, nevertheless,I will not ceaseTo sing, by by, lullay."

The child then spake; in his talking he to his mother said,—"I bekid[K] am king, in crib though I be laid;For angels brightDown to me light,Thou knowest it is no nay,And of that sightThou mayest be lightTo sing, by by, lullay."

"Now, sweet Son, since thou art king, why art thou laid in stall?Why not thou ordain thy bedding in some great kingès hall?Methinketh it is rightThat king or knightShould be in good array;And them amongIt were no wrongTo sing, by by, lullay."

"Mary, mother, I am thy child, though I be laid in stall,Lords and dukes shall worship me and so shall kingès all.Ye shall well seeThat kingès threeShall come on the twelfth day;For this behestGive me thy breastAnd sing, by by, lullay."

"Now tell me, sweet Son, I thee pray, thou art my love and dear,How should I keep thee to thy pay[L] and make thee glad of cheer?For all thy willI would fulfilThou weet'st full well in fay,And for all thisI will thee kiss,And sing, by by, lullay."

"My dear mother, when time it be, take thou me up aloft, And set me upon thy knee and handle me full soft. And in thy arm Thou wilt me warm, And keep me night and day; If I weep And may not sleep Thou sing, by by, lullay."

"Now, sweet Son, since it is so, all things are at thy will, I pray thee grant to me a boon if it be right and skill, That child or man, That will or can, Be merry upon my day; To bliss them bring, And I shall sing, Lullay, by by, lullay."

FOOTNOTES:

[I] Endris night: last night.

[J] Hay.

[K] Nevertheless.

[L] Peace.

A ROCKING HYMN.

Sweet baby, sleep; what ails my dear?What ails my darling thus to cry?Be still, my child, and lend thine earTo hear me sing thy lullaby.My pretty lamb, forbear to weep;Be still, my dear; sweet baby, sleep.

Thou blessed soul, what canst thou fear?What things to thee can mischief do?Thy God is now thy Father dear;His holy Spouse thy Mother, too.Sweet baby, then, forbear to weep;Be still, my babe; sweet baby, sleep.

Whilst thus thy lullaby I sing,For thee great blessings ripening be;Thine eldest brother is a king,And hath a kingdom bought for thee.Sweet baby, then, forbear to weep;Be still, my babe; sweet baby, sleep.

Sweet baby, sleep, and nothing fear,For whosoever thee offends,By thy protector threatened are,And God and angels are thy friends.Sweet baby, then, forbear to weep;Be still, my babe; sweet baby, sleep.

When God with us was dwelling here,In little babes he took delight:Such innocents as thou, my dear,Are ever precious in his sight.Sweet baby, then, forbear to weep;Be still, my babe; sweet baby, sleep.

A little infant once was he,And Strength-in-Weakness then was laidupon his Virgin-Mother's knee,That power to thee might be conveyed.Sweet baby, then, forbear to weep;Be still, my babe; sweet baby, sleep.

In this thy frailty and thy needHe friends and helpers doth prepare,Which thee shall cherish, clothe, and feed,For of thy weal they tender are.Sweet baby, then, forbear to weep;Be still, my babe; sweet baby, sleep.

The King of kings, when he was born,Had not so much for outward ease;By him such dressings were not worn,Nor such-like swaddling-clothes as these.Sweet baby, then, forbear to weep;Be still, my babe; sweet baby, sleep.

Within a manger lodged thy Lord,Where oxen lay and asses fed;Warm rooms we do to thee afford,An easy cradle or a bed.Sweet baby, then, forbear to weep;Be still, my babe; sweet baby, sleep.

The wants that he did then sustainHave purchased wealth, my babe, for thee,And by his torments and his painThy rest and ease secured be.My baby, then, forbear to weep;Be still, my babe; sweet baby, sleep.

Thou hast (yet more), to perfect this,A promise and an earnest gotOf gaining everlasting bliss,Though thou, my babe, perceiv'st it not.Sweet baby, then, forbear to weep;Be still, my babe; sweet baby, sleep.

George Wither.

A CRADLE-SONG OF THE VIRGIN.

The Virgin stills the cryingOf Jesus, sleepless lying;And singing for his pleasure,Thus calls upon her treasure,"My darling, do not weep, my Jesu, sleep!"

O lamb, my love inviting,O star, my soul delighting,O flower of mine own bearing,O jewel past comparing!My darling, etc.

My Child, of might indwelling,My sweet, all sweets excelling,Of bliss the fountain flowing,The dayspring ever glowingMy darling, etc.

My joy, my exultation,My spirit's consolation;My son, my spouse, my brother,O listen to thy mother!My darling, etc.

Say, would'st thou heavenly sweetness,Or love of answering meetness?Or is fit music wanting?Ho! angels, raise your chanting!My darling, etc.

Translated from the Latin by Rev. H. R. Bramley.

WHISPERING PALMS.

Holy angels and blest, Through these Palms as ye sweep, Hold their branches at rest, For my Babe is asleep.

And ye, Bethlehem palm-trees, As stormy winds rush In tempest and fury Your angry noise hush;—Move gently, move gently, Restrain your wild sweep; Hold your branches at rest—My Babe is asleep.

Lope de Vega.

A CHRISTMAS LULLABY.

Sleep, baby, sleep! The Mother sings;Heaven's angels kneel and fold their wings:Sleep, baby, sleep!

With swathes of scented hay thy bedBy Mary's hand at eve was spread.Sleep, baby, sleep!

At midnight came the shepherds, theyWhom seraphs wakened by the way.Sleep, baby, sleep!

And three kings from the East afarEre dawn came, guided by thy star.Sleep, baby, sleep!

They brought thee gifts of gold and gems,Pure orient pearls, rich diadems.Sleep, baby, sleep!

But thou who liest slumbering there,Art King of kings, earth, ocean, air.Sleep, baby, sleep!

Sleep, baby, sleep! The shepherds sing:Through heaven, through earth, hosannas ring.Sleep, baby, sleep!

John Addington Symonds.

THE VIRGIN'S CRADLE-HYMN.

Dormi, Jesu! Mater ridetQuæ tam dulcem somnum videt,Dormi, Jesu! blandule!Si non dormis, Mater ploratInter fila cantans orat,Blande, veni, somnule.

Translation.

Sleep, sweet babe! my cares beguiling:Mother sits beside thee smiling;Sleep, my darling, tenderly!If thou sleep not, mother mourneth,Singing as her wheel she turneth:Come soft slumber, balmily!

Samuel Taylor Coleridge.

THE SOVEREIGN.

Upon my lap my sovereign sitsAnd sucks upon my breast;Meantime his love maintains my lifeAnd gives my sense her rest.Sing lullaby, my little boy,Sing lullaby, mine only joy!

When thou hast taken thy repast,Repose, my babe, on me;So may thy mother and thy nurseThy cradle also be..Sing lullaby, my little boy,Sing lullaby, mine only joy!

I grieve that duty doth not workAll that my wishing would,Because I would not be to theeBut in the best I should.Sing lullaby, my little boy,Sing lullaby, mine only joy!

Yet as I am, and as I mayI must and will be thine,Though all too little for thyselfVouchsafing to be mine.Sing lullaby, my little boy,Sing lullaby, mine only joy!

Martin Peerson, a.d. 1620.

BY THE CRADLE-SIDE.

Sweet dreams, form a shadeO'er my lovely infant's head!Sweet dreams of pleasant streamsBy happy, silent, moony beams!

Sweet sleep, with soft downWeave thy brows an infant crown!Sweet sleep, angel mild,Hover o'er my happy child!

Sweet smiles, in the nightHover over my delight!Sweet smiles, mother's smileAll the livelong night beguile.

Sweet moans, dovelike sighs,Chase not slumber from thine eyes!Sweet moan, sweeter smile,All the dovelike moans beguile!

Sleep, sleep, happy child!All creation slept and smiled.Sleep, sleep, happy sleep,While o'er thee doth mother weep.

Sweet babe, in thy faceHoly image I can trace;Sweet babe, once like theeThy Maker lay and wept for me:

Wept for me, for thee, for all,When he was an infant small;Thou his image ever see,Heavenly face that smiles on thee!

Smiles on thee, on me, on all,Who became an infant small,Infant smiles are his own smiles:Heaven and earth to peace beguiles.

William Blake.

THE VIRGIN MARY TO THE CHILD JESUS.

But see, the Virgin blestHath laid her babe to rest.

Milton.

I.

Sleep, sleep, mine Holy One!My flesh, my Lord!—what name? I do not knowA name that seemeth not too high or low,Too far from me or heaven.My Jesus, that is best! that word being givenBy the majestic angel whose commandWas softly as a man's beseeching said,When I and all the earth appeared to standIn the great overflowOf light celestial from his wings and head.Sleep, sleep, my saving One!

II.

And art Thou come for saving, baby-browedAnd speechless Being—art Thou come for saving?The palm that grows beside our door is bowedBy treadings of the low wind from the south,A restless shadow through the chamber waving:Upon its bough a bird sings in the sun;But Thou, with that close slumber on thy mouth,Dost seem of wind and sun already weary.Art come for saving, O my weary One?

III.

Perchance this sleep that shutteth out the drearyEarth-sounds and motions, opens on Thy soulHigh dreams on fire with God;High songs that make the pathways where they rollMore bright than stars do theirs; and visions newOf Thine eternal nature's old abode.Suffer this mother's kiss,Best thing that earthly is,To guide the music and the glory through,Nor narrow in Thy dream the broad upliftingsOf any seraph wing!Thus, noiseless, thus. Sleep, sleep, my dreaming One!

IV.

The slumber of His lips meseems to runThrough my lips to mine heart; to all its shiftingsOf sensual life, bring contrariousnessIn a great calm. I feel, I could lie downAs Moses did, and die, [M]— and then live most.I am 'ware of you, heavenly Presences,That stand with your peculiar light unlost,Each forehead with a high thought for a crown,Unsunned i' the sunshine! I am 'ware. Yet throwNo shade against the wall! How motionlessYe round me with your living statuary,While through your whiteness, in and outwardly,Continual thoughts of God appear to go,Like light's soul in itself! I bear, I bear,To look upon the dropt lids of your eyes,Though their external shining testifiesTo that beatitude within, which wereEnough to blast an eagle at his sun.I fall not on my sad clay face before ye;I look on His. I knowMy spirit which dilateth with the woeOf His mortality,May well contain your glory.Yea, drop your lids more low,Ye are but fellow-worshippers with me!Sleep, sleep, my worshipped One!

V.

We sate among the stalls at Bethlehem.The dumb kine from their fodder turning them,Softened their horned facesTo almost human gazesTowards the newly born.The simple shepherds from the star-lit brooksBrought visionary looks,As yet in their astonished hearing rungThe strange, sweet angel-tongue.The magi of the East, in sandals worn,Knelt reverent, sweeping round,With long pale beards their gifts upon the ground,The incense, myrrh and gold,These baby hands were impotent to hold.So, let all earthlies and celestials waitUpon thy royal state!Sleep, sleep, my kingly One!

VI.

I am not proud—meek angels, ye investNew meeknesses to hear such utterance restOn mortal lips,—"I am not proud"—not proud!Albeit in my flesh God sent His Son,Albeit over Him my head is bowedAs others bow before Him, still mine heartBows lower than their knees. O centuriesThat roll, in vision, your futuritiesMy future grave athwart,—Whose murmurs seem to reach me while I keepWatch o'er this sleep,—Say of me as the heavenly said,—"Thou artThe blessedest of women!"—blessedest,Not holiest, not noblest,—no high name,Whose height misplaced may pierce me like a shame,When I sit meek in heaven!

VII.

For me—for me—God knows that I am feeble like the rest!—I often wandered forth, more child than maiden,Among the midnight hills of Galilee,Whose summits looked heaven-laden;Listening to silence as it seemed to beGod's voice, so soft yet strong—so fain to press upon my heart as heaven did on the height, And waken up its shadows by a light, And show its vileness by a holiness. Then I knelt down most silent like the night, Too self-renounced for fears, Raising my small face to the boundless blue Whose stars did mix and tremble in my tears. God heard them falling after—with His dew.

VIII.

So, seeing my corruption, can I see. This Incorruptible now born of me This fair new Innocence no sun did chance To shine on, (for even Adam was no child,) Created from my nature all defiled, This mystery from out mine ignorance—Nor feel the blindness, stain, corruption, more Than others do, or I did heretofore?—Can hands wherein such burden pure has been, Not open with the cry, "Unclean, unclean!" More oft than any else beneath the skies? Ah King, ah Christ, ah Son! The kine, the shepherds, the abased wise, Must all less lowly wait Than I, upon thy state!—Sleep, sleep, my kingly One!

IX.

Art Thou a King, then? Come, His universe, Come, crown me Him a king! Pluck rays from all such stars as never fling Their light where fell a curse. And make a crowning for this kingly brow!—What is my word?—Each empyreal star Sits in a sphere afar In shining ambuscade: The child-brow, crowned by none, Keeps its unchildlike shade. Sleep, sleep, my crownless One!

X.

Unchildlike shade!—no other babe doth wearAn aspect very sorrowful, as Thou.—No small babe-smiles, my watching heart has seen,To float like speech the speechless lips between;No dovelike cooing in the golden air,No quick short joys of leaping babyhood.Alas, our earthly goodIn heaven thought evil, seems too good for Thee:Yet, sleep, my weary One!

XI.

And then the drear, sharp tongue of prophecy,With the dread sense of things which shall be done,Doth smite me inly, like a sword—a sword?—(That "smites the Shepherd!") then I think aloudThe words "despised,"—"rejected,"—every wordRecoiling into darkness as I viewThe darling on my knee.Bright angels,—move not!—lest ye stir the cloudBetwixt my soul and His futurity!I must not die, with mother's work to do,And could not live—and see.

XII.

It is enough to bearThis image still and fair—This holier in sleep,Than a saint at prayer:This aspect of a childWho never sinned or smiled—This presence in an infant's face:This sadness most like love,This love than love more deep,This weakness like omnipotence,It is so strong to move!Awful is this watching place,Awful what I see from hence—A king, without regalia,A God, without the thunder,A child, without the heart for play;Ay, a Creator rent asunderFrom His first glory and cast awayOn His own world, for me aloneTo hold in hands created, crying—Son!

XIII.

That tear fell not on TheeBeloved, yet Thou stirrest in Thy slumber!Thou, stirring not for glad sounds out of number Which through the vibratory palm-trees runFrom summer wind and bird,So quickly hast Thou heardA tear fall silently?—Wak'st Thou, O loving One?

Elizabeth Barrett Browning.

FOOTNOTE:

[M]It is a Jewish tradition that Moses died of the kisses of God's lips.

A BEDSIDE DITTY.

Baby, baby dear, Earth and heaven are near Now, for heaven is here.

Heaven is every place Where your flower-sweet face Fills our eyes with grace.

Till your own eyes deign Earth a glance again, Earth and heaven are twain.

Now your sleep is done, Shine, and show the sun Earth and heaven are one.

Algernon Charles Swinburne.

GIVEN BACK ON CHRISTMAS MORN.

(A MOTHER WATCHES BY HER SICK BABE.)

Round about the casementWail the winds of winter;Shaken from the frozen eavesMany an icy splinter.On the hillside, in the hollow,Weaving wreaths of snow:Now in gusts of solemn musicLost in murmurs low;Howling now across the woldIn its shroudlike vastness,Like the wolves about a foldIn some Alpine fastness,Hungered by the cold.

(THE MOTHER SINGS.)

Babe of mine—babe of mine,Must I lose you?Dare I weep if the DivineWill should choose you?—Ah, to mourn, as I have smiled,At the thought of you, my child!Ah, my child—my child!

Babe of mine—you entwineWith existence!If one strips the clinging vineThere's resistance—Shall not I then——? I talk wild,Seeing Death so near my child:—Ah, my child—my child!

Babe of mine—heart's best wine—Life's pure essence!Gloomy shadows, that defineDeath's near presence.Dim those dear eyes, undefiledAs God's violets—ah, my child:Ah, my child—my child!

The imperial purple of the nightIs spread, wine-dark, above,But glistens with no gems of light,To hint of Heaven's love.A sombre pall hangs overhead,Fringed with lurid clouds of lead,—O'er the sleeping earth belowOne long, wide waste of silent snow,And the wind moans drearilyAs it wanders by,And the night wanes wearilyIn the starlight sky.

167

(THE MOTHER SINGS.)

Must the dear eyes close?Must the lips be still?—How I love their speech that flowsLike a wanton rill!Must those cheeks, soft-tinged with rose,Pallid grow and chill?Give her back to me, angel in disguise!So your mystery I shall learn—yet with tearless eyes.By the pangs, the prayers,By the mother's glee,By her hopes, her fears, her cares,Give my child to me—Give it back to me!

Quenched the eye's soft light,Hushed the cowslip breath!Going, darling, in the night?Spare—oh, spare her, Death!Dying—is it so?Oh, it must not be!Can my one poor treasure go?Give her back to me,Give her back to me:Or take me too,—left alone,Now my little one is gone;Ah, my child, my child!

Among the clouds that sail o'erheadA yellow radiance is shed;And o'er the hill-tops wrapt in snow,Is born a tinge of rosy glow.Within the air a stir—like wingsOf angels in their minist'rings;A tremulous motion, and a thrill,As with faint light the heavens fill.Night's sombre clouds are slow withdrawn,And nature cries, Awake, 'tis dawn.

About the lonely casementBlows fresh the breath of day;—The mother, in amazement,Sees death-glooms fade away!

The blue eyes open once again,Once more the lips have smiled—Her tears fell like the spring-time rain:God gives her back her child!

Hush, there are footsteps on the snow,That pause the lattice-pane below;While voices chant the carol-rhymes,The Christmas song of olden times:

Awake, good Christians! Long agoThe shepherds waked at nightAnd saw the heavens with glory glow,And angels in the light.Hosanna! sing, Hosanna! sing,Hosanna in the height!

New life they told to all on earth,New life and blessing bright,Forewarning of the Saviour's birth,In Bethlehem this night.Hosanna! sing, Hosanna! sing,Hosanna in the height!

New life to all,—new life to all,—The tidings good recite!New life to all, which did befallAt Bethlehem this night.Hosanna! sing, Hosanna! sing,Hosanna in the height!

The voices hushed—the footsteps diedIn distance far aloof,It seemed a blessing did abideUpon that silent roof,As far away their cheery singingUpon the frosty air came ringing.

Among the clouds that sail o'erheadA yellow glory is outspread;And on the hill-tops crowned with snows,A rosy blushing radiance grows,As wider still the warm light glows:And flooding daylight falls againFrom cloud to hill—from hill to plain.

A golden sea of swimming lightPoured o'er the sombre shores of night,While the glad mother, to her breastHer child yet close and closer pressed,Her rescued treasure—newly born—Her babe—given back on Christmas morn.

Thomas Hood.

A LULLING SONG.

Hush! my dear, lie still and slumber, Holy Angels guard thy bed; Heavenly blessings without number Gently falling on thy head.

Sleep, my babe; thy food and raiment, House and home, thy friends provide; All without thy care or payment, All thy wants are well supplied.

How much better thou'rt attended Than the Son of God could be, When from heaven He descended, And became a child like thee!

Soft and easy is thy cradle: Coarse and hard thy Saviour lay, When His birthplace was a stable, And His softest bed was hay.

See the kinder shepherds round Him, Telling wonders from the sky! Where they sought Him, there they found Him With His Virgin-Mother by.

See the lovely Babe a-dressing; Lovely Infant, how He smiled! When He wept, the Mother's blessing Soothed and hush'd the holy Child.

Lo, He slumbers in His manger, Where the hornéd oxen fed;— Peace, my darling, here's no danger; Here's no ox a-near thy bed!

May'st thou live to know and fear Him, Trust and love Him all thy days; Then go dwell forever near Him, See His face and sing His praise!

I could give thee thousand kisses, Hoping what I most desire; Not a mother's fondest wishesCan to greater joys aspire.

Isaac Watts.

GOOD-NIGHT.

Good-night, good-night, the day is done;Rock, rock the cradle, little one;The lamp is low, and low the sun,Good-night!

Good-night, good-night, the Christmas boughBends to the rocking wind, and thouTo mother's ditty noddest now,Good-night!

Good-night, good-night, the holy dayBring baby sweets, and sweets alway!Rock, rock—then, tiptoe, steal away,Good-night!

H. S. M.

END OF BOOK III.

The End

www.ingramcontent.com/pod-product-compliance
Lightning Source LLC
Chambersburg PA
CBHW070651290526
45790CB00001B/269